THE TURNING TIDE
BY
BRENDA ROBSON

MARSHALL·PICKERING

Marshall Pickering
34–42 Cleveland Street, London. W1P 5FB. U.K.

Copyright © 1989 Brenda Robson

First published 1989 by Marshall Morgan and Scott Publications Ltd
Part of the Marshall Pickering Holdings Group

All rights reserved. No part of this publication may be reproduced, stored in a retrieval system, or transmitted, in any form or by any means, electronic, mechanical, photocopying, recording or otherwise, without the permission in writing, of the publisher.

British Library Cataloguing in Publication Data
Robson, Brenda
   The Turning Tide.
   1. Christian church. Role of women
   I. Title
262'.15

ISBN 0-551-01897-6

Scripture quotations in this publication are from the Holy Bible, New International Version. Copyright © 1973, 1978, 1984 International Bible Society. Published in the U.K. by Hodder and Stoughton.

Text Set in Bembo by Selectmove Ltd, London
Printed in Great Britain by Cox & Wyman

Contents

Forewords	: John Noble and Dave Tomlinson	(v)
Introduction	: What's it all about?	(ix)
Chapter 1	: From the beginning	11
Chapter 2	: By default or design?	23
Chapter 3	: Against the odds	46
Chapter 4	: Issues need not divide us	63
Chapter 5	: Breaking the mould	74
Chapter 6	: Our history. . . .	92
Chapter 7	: . . . .Our destiny	102
Chapter 8	: Every man, Every woman	113
Postscript	:	121
Bibliography:		126

Acknowledgments

Thank you to Guildford Community Church for trusting me to lead you, and to my close friends for your love, care and support. Without you I would not have been able to fulfil the many tasks that God has given me to do.

I want to express my appreciation to Jan Luft for tapping seemingly endless words into the computer, and Derek Poole, Jane Hepburn, Rod Boreham and Martyn Whiteman who have assisted me with the script.

I am particularly grateful to our church team, a terrific crew, Pete Brayne, Andy McKenzie, Pauline Boland, Andy Jones, Pat French and Philip Vogel, who have given encouragement when needed. Thanks also to my niece, Biz Robson who lives with me and has put up with much groaning!

Finally, my thanks to the French family, especially Pat and Anna, and to Terry Brewer and others close to me who have inspired courage in me to believe in God and in myself.

Forewords

We 'house church people' like to think of ourselves as being fairly radical, and I suppose in some ways we are, but in lots of other areas, we're surprisingly conservative – in our attitudes toward women in leadership for example. Yes, it's true that some house churches are pursuing a policy of equal opportunities for men and women, but they are still few and far between. Despite the sustained delay in the ordination of women in the Anglican church in the U.K., there's probably still more scope for women to express their gifts in the institutional church than in the average house church.

Brenda Robson is a demonstration, however, that the tide is turning. Even in the face of discouragement and opposition she has mustered the courage and self confidence to persist in the calling God has given her, and she's not alone. All over the land women in all kinds of churches are daring to believe that their gifts of leadership, preaching and teaching have a valid place in the mainstream of church life. It can only be a matter of time before many more of them are granted full opportunity to function freely. Churches bold enough to opt for true biblical partnership between the sexes will increasingly be models for others to observe and from whom to learn.

Of course, I'm not naïve enough to think that the biblical debate will not continue (probably indefinitely), and I have full sympathy with those who struggle over the difficult exegetical and hermeneutical issues. I myself wrestled with them for around three years before settling on the legitimacy of female leadership in the church. One thing that I do believe very strongly is that it is vital that women are afforded the freedom we men have had for centuries to make their mistakes without dozens of people jumping down their throats and saying, 'There you are, we told you leadership wasn't for women.' In this book

Brenda shares frankly and freely some of her weaknesses and her mistakes since she took on leadership and I hope many women will be encouraged by her vulnerability and humanness.

One thing which is apparent from Brenda's writing is her fervent desire for real partnership rather than male displacement. The anger and bitterness of women who have been dispossessed of rights and treated harshly can be understood, but the Christian response to sexual and other forms of prejudice is surely to work towards repentance, reconciliation and a full working partnership, rather than opting for a mere exchange of power.

I'm sure this book isn't offered as a major theological work and I doubt if it will convince the cynical biblicist; but it is a moving expression of a person struggling against the tide, when disadvantaged not only by being a woman in a very male domain, but also by being single into the bargain. It seems a tragedy to me that the church is one of the very few sections of the community where there is exemption from laws governing sexual discrimination.

I believe Christian women have a mission in this world which begins right in the church itself: to bring the all too often neglected dimensions of humanity which we call femininity. Most sections of our society are dominated by male perspectives and values. We desperately need women who will work in equal partnership with men and yet still dare to be women and thus help to bring some of the healing and balance society so badly craves.

I hope this book encourages women to humbly, yet firmly, grasp the opportunities now arising, and I pray it will trigger repentance on the part of those men who have deliberately or inadvertently frustrated the purpose of God being outworked through their sisters.

Dave Tomlinson
May 1989

* * *

Foreword

I first met Bren Robson some years ago at a leaders conference which had been arranged by Team Spirit, the ministry team for which I am responsible. I was impressed by her willingness to venture outside of her own secure circle of relationships in order to build bridges and see if there were other perspectives from which she could learn. Our hearts were knit together by the Holy Spirit and it was not long before we were exploring the possibilities of working together in the team along with Terry Brewer and Phil Vogel, who were also part of the leadership at Guildford Community Church at that time.

Ultimately GCC, along with their leaders, agreed to release Bren, Terry and Phil to work part of their time in the wider church here in the UK and overseas through Team Spirit. This they did without withdrawing or even reducing the remuneration which each one was receiving. I believe they saw this move as a means of giving some of the very best which they possessed to their brothers and sisters in other parts of this country and the world. Their decision was not only generous, but was a prophetic statement, first about giving and second about the way men and women can work side by side in harmony to lead and influence others.

Their action was also a demonstration of Christian love and tolerance. You see, not all of the thirty or so men and women who make up Team Spirit are agreed about the extent to which women can take responsibility in the church. However, having been totally open with one another, we came to the conclusion that our unity and relationships were more important than our differences. In this climate we have learned to respect one another's opinions and work within the boundaries which love demands as we cross over into one another's churches or areas of responsibility. In view of the intensity of the burden which Bren carries to see that women achieve their full potential, it is a credit to her patience and submissive heart that she gladly accepts these limitations knowing that change, and the speed with which it comes, is a work of the Holy Spirit and not merely the result of human initiation.

For these reasons alone I would be keen to encourage Christians who are seeking to understand the issues surrounding women's ministry and leadership in the church, to study what she has to say. However, in addition, I believe you will find *The Turning Tide* to be a helpful combination of experience and discovery without attempting to cover the subject in detail. The bibliography should provide all the necessary information for those who wish to pursue other aspects of this vital topic. I am so happy to endorse a book which has content, is easy to read and comes from a trusted friend and co-worker.

John Noble
Team Spirit
Romford
Essex

Introduction – What's It All About?

Despite numerous publications on the subject of the role of women in the church, it would seem that thousands are still struggling to find their place in the Christian community and striving to believe that they have anything valuable to contribute.

Lack of self-esteem and personal value is a universal epidemic contagious to both sexes, but I believe it is more keenly experienced by women. *The Turning Tide* is an account of the difficulties, anxieties and pain I experienced in coming to terms with an apparently misplaced leadership gift and the need to develop a positive self-image and sense of personal worth. It is also an account of the variety of people whose encouragement has enriched and strengthened my pilgrimage. I have written these pages with ordinary men and women in mind who may identify with similar struggles, in the hope of inspiring courage in them.

This book is not another attempt to accommodate the reactionary attitudes of radical feminism. For me the key issue, as in any other area of life, is to hear what God is saying. I believe that it is King Jesus, the future Bridegroom of the church who is drawing our attention to the place of women, in our society, in the world and in the church.

Over the years, I have had to understand and resolve seven major areas, both emotionally and intellectually, the essence of which makes up the chapters of this book.

1: From The Beginning

From a very early age I have been aware of divine intervention in my life and of particular purposes God has for me to fulfil. Humanly speaking I am not the best material for church leadership. I am single, a woman and have a traumatic personal history. Consequently I would hardly be an obvious choice to help pioneer a course for women within a male dominated world. God sees me from a different perspective. His strength in my weakness has become more than just a theological cliché – it is truth being realised.

I was born in the north east of England, near the Scottish border, into an environment that was, and which to a large extent still is, a man's world. We were a close-knit farming community which men dominated. Our livelihood depended upon the men, they ran everything. Women were not expected to be present at important events such as the livestock auctions and farm sales. They were generally excluded from drinking clubs, sporting occasions, and arenas where relationships were made and important decisions taken; and if by chance a woman did appear on these occasions, it would have been regarded as extremely strange.

There were very clear divisions between what was expected of men and women. In many homes men would always be served first at meal times. When they returned from work, wives would be expected to stop what they were doing and look after their husbands, or grown-up sons. They would come in from a hard day in the fields, slump in a chair, and expect to be waited on hand and foot. Men to me seemed to be very demanding, expecting life to revolve around them, their whims and moods being catered for in their time and at their pace.

Drinking and public houses were men's territory; church and tea parties were considered more appropriate for women. The local vicar was treated with scorn because of the funny clothes that he wore. He was not like the real, working men.

A woman did all the shopping. It was her job. Men would rarely be seen washing the dishes, cooking or changing nappies; after all, physical strength, and the ability to use it, was the all-important factor as far as the men were concerned. Strength was equated with maturity and masculinity; if you were not strong, you were either a child or a woman. The finer emotions had to be suppressed and kept well out of sight; any display of emotion, especially weeping, was regarded as immature, childish and weak. I can remember many times as children we were ridiculed and laughed at for crying, adults would say 'Stop that nonsense, run away and play.'

It was very important for married couples to have a son first. A son would take precedence with regard to education, vocation and inheritance even if they had a daughter first. It was all-important to have someone to carry on the family name. A son was vital.

Girls received little encouragement to pursue a career, except perhaps teaching or nursing. Their job was cooking, mending, and serving the men. Boys, on the other hand, were urged to better themselves, to achieve educational success and financial status. Young women were often little more than sex symbols to be whistled at and taunted as men chose. Without good looks a woman was unlikely to find a husband

and the security this was seen to bring in our rural community.

Simple things highlighted the status of the sexes. Men always drove the family car and would sit together with their son in the front seats, whilst mother and daughter were consigned to the back. It would be fair to say that, in many families, once a son had reached maturity, he replaced his mother in terms of importance in the family. Daughters often lost out completely. It was not until I eventually came to the south of England, to boarding school, that I realised this was not the case everywhere. For the first eleven years of my life, however, the male dominated environment was all that I knew, and I could not imagine anything different.

Throughout the majority of my childhood I lived with the thought that I was a mis-conception. I was not planned and I grew up aware of this, with strong feelings of rejection filling my heart. These feelings were further compounded by the fact that at the age of two I underwent emergency surgery for the removal of a tumour behind my right eye. This in itself was traumatic enough, but in those days it was considered better for parents not to see their children until they had fully recovered. I was confused, bewildered and felt very alone, unable at such a young age to understand what was happening to me. Although I knew that my life was threatened because I had heard people discussing my case, I did not know what was wrong with me. As far as I was concerned my parents were gone forever. I had no awareness that they would ever return, and death seemed to stare me in the face. There was no understanding at that time that children could be affected by such things, even if they could not talk about them. The idea that a child could be suffering intense emotional upheaval and pain through such an experience was not entertained.

The surgeons were unsure as to whether they had caught the tumour in time. There was always the possibility of secondary tumours having formed in my body. Life itself seemed uncertain and from my viewpoint remained this way for many years. Doctors had no choice but to operate and remove the tumour, and my right eye with it. Some years later I was told by a physician of some standing that eye surgery is the most traumatic of all for children to undergo. Before the development of conceptual thinking, sight is all a child has; the present is all important. If the visual image is removed, life itself is perceived to be under threat.

Eventually, of course, I realised that I was not going to die. The removal of my right eye, however, not only changed my appearance physically, but left me with deep emotional wounds which remained hidden for many years. I was ashamed of how I looked, at first with a patch over my eye, then a clear shell replacement and eventually a proper eye. I never even looked in a mirror until days before going to my first school because I was much too frightened of what I might see. Throughout that entire period, I developed the habit of walking around with my hand over my eye, so that no-one could see what was wrong. I spent many hours pacing up and down our garden at home, desperately afraid that someone would come and take me away again.

It was not until I was twelve that I knew for sure my life was out of danger. Up to that point there was a constant threat that my left eye too could have been damaged by the tumour, and that I might be totally blind. Until I was given the all-clear from the hospital I had no assurance that I was going to survive.

Throughout my childhood I lived in the midst of rage and aggression. The atmosphere at home was often very tense because of longstanding clashes between different sides of the wider family. At times emotions were so highly charged that I feared for my own safety. My only recourse was to escape to the hills alone, for it was there that I felt safe and secure.

After successfully taking the 11 plus examination, I was eligible to attend the nearest grammar school, some twenty miles away. The distance made this prospect rather impractical but, there was still a chance that I could board. I was determined to change my environment but despite my efforts at the interview to influence the panel that I should board, I was told the places were full. I had done a good job of persuasion, however, because a few days later my parents were sent a list of other boarding schools to look at. I scoured the list myself and chose a school in the South-East of England. My parents seemed happy enough to leave the choice to me, and could afford the fees because I had won a part scholarship. I left for my new school which even then raised hopes within me of a new beginning. Little did I realise that this was to herald one of the greatest traumas of all.

Coming as I did from a small community, hidden among the bleak Pennine hills, where everybody knew me and what I had been through, I was completely lost. When I arrived in the affluent south-east, I was just one of many. The size of the school and the number of pupils was overwhelming. There seemed to be an endless maze of corridors, enormous halls and countless classrooms. I knew nobody, had never met any of the pupils before, and stood out like a sore thumb because of my broad northern accent. I made sure I soon corrected that! I knew nothing about the finer points of life such as elegant manners and etiquette and even in this respect I was also different from the majority of pupils.

In the first year I experienced what can only be described as culture shock. Even the number of books in the school bothered me. At home we had never had enough money to buy books, and I was not allowed to borrow books from the library on the grounds that books 'contained germs'! Now here I was faced with a veritable mountain of life threatening germs! I just could not believe the quantity of reading material that was available.

The most critical part of adjusting was perhaps to do with the fact that my appearance was different to that of everyone else. The eye operation had not only left me with a man-made replacement, but had also affected some of the muscles on the right side of my face, so that the area underneath my right eye began to droop. I was acutely aware of this problem, and of people's reactions to it. Not until I received plastic surgery at the age of thirteen was my suffering relieved.

To add to my feelings of fear and loss, I also felt I had no one to turn to for help. My fear turned to aggression, which made it all the more difficult for me to relate to others and they to me. I was not able to go out and play by myself as I had been used to, and found myself shut up in a large dormitory of girls I did not want to be with. After about a year of ups and downs I had begun to form some close relationships, and this helped me more than anything else to adjust. Gradually I realised that some of my own age group were going through similar traumas, one of them a coloured girl who began to share how alienated she felt in an all white school. Slowly I found a few friends with whom I could identify and eventually risked trusting them enough to share my own feelings of isolation and loneliness.

I felt the pressure to do well at school was enormous. I had learnt in all kinds of different ways that to be of value in life I must succeed. My education was being paid for and I could not therefore, contemplate failure. As a result I succumbed to the temptation of exaggerating my achievements, though school reports soon uncovered the true situation!

As time went on I got used to life in the south, and tried harder, eventually starting to do well in most areas of school life. The highlight came when I was top of my year in the exams and got into the 'A' stream. Despite this climb to reasonable success, however, an aching emptiness still remained within me which academic achievements did not fill.

As a child I possessed only two books, one of which was a rather tatty illustrated Bible. On many occasions I would stare at the pictures of Jesus and imagine what it must have been like to have been there with him. When I was nine one of my cousins helped introduce me to Jesus. He had just returned from a theology course at Cliff College and, in northern opinion, had 'gone overboard with all this religion'. On cold winter nights he would drive around farms in his Land Rover, inviting all the children to come and have supper with him. This turned out to be a trip to the local vicarage, where the vicar would supply food and the challenge of the gospel.

On one such occasion I decided I had nothing better to do, and was glad of the opportunity to get out of the house, so agreed to go along. I clambered into the Land Rover along with all the other kids, and was soon being whisked down country lanes in the darkness to our supper date with the vicar. The image of a very old man is firmly fixed in my imagination, although in truth the vicar was probably no more than forty-five! He told us the story of Jesus and assured us that He was alive now. He then explained what would happen if we gave Him our hearts and although I didn't really understand what it would entail, I asked Jesus into my life with the limited understanding that I had. I was given a card which I have to this day, confirming the step that I had taken.

Somehow I understood that if I knew Jesus I was supposed to be a good girl. I tried to be good, but never succeeded for very long. From those early years, however, I was somehow aware of a destiny upon my life. I would preach to my mother from my tatty Bible, standing behind a rickety table which I had covered with a white cloth, thus transforming it into an altar. With hindsight I can see that God was already planting his desires for my life within me. Between the planting of those desires and their fulfilment, however, were years of searching and disillusionment.

When I first went to junior school in the north I lied about my eye to some of my friends. So desperate was I to look like all the other children, that I told them I was going to America for an eye transplant. Not long after my decision at the vicarage, however, I became aware that Jesus performed miracles and healed people. This stirred my imagination and began to raise hopes that He could do something for me. One summer's night, as the evening rays of the sun filtered through my bedroom window, I looked at myself in the mirror and told Jesus how I felt about the way I looked. I did not like what I saw, and was fairly straight with Him. By the time I woke up I wanted a new eye please! I really believed that I would get one, and went to bed feeling quite happy. When I awoke the next morning to discover that a new eye had not appeared, I decided that all of this 'christian stuff' did not work. I was very disappointed and disenchanted and gave up all attempts to follow Jesus for a long time.

After boarding school I went to college in London. The deep emptiness inside was still there but I ignored it for the most part as I sought to find enjoyment and fulfilment in social life. Eventually I became seriously involved in one relationship to the point of contemplating marriage. But this friendship, though intimate, did not satisfy my need for love. I attempted to ignore how I felt and made sure that I kept myself occupied. When alone, I was conscious of feeling anxious and restless for no particular reason and often paced my college floor unable to sleep. In those days I felt an ache inside, and whilst I was unaware of it's cause, I can see now I was longing to be cherished and cared for. I had caught a glimpse of that kind of loving when, at nine, I had realised for the first time that Jesus was my Father. It was probably this which occasionally drove me to attend church services. I tried a few to see what they could offer, but did not find what I was looking for. Whatever was missing in my life, the church did not seem to hold the vital ingredient.

One evening I was challenged by a friend to go to a particular church where a preacher was reputedly packing them in. 'You'll be lucky to get a seat,' he assured me. I found it difficult to believe, but out of curiosity went to Commercial Road Baptist Church in Guildford to hear David Pawson. When I arrived outside the building, there was a notice on the door saying 'Church Full'. In utter disbelief I walked up the steps to the entrance and because I was a visitor, was squeezed in. To my amazement the building was packed to the doors. As soon as David Pawson stood to lead the meeting and preach, I knew that he had whatever it was I had been searching for.

Over a period of six months I became increasingly drawn to God. I came to realise that Jesus not only wanted to be my Saviour, but He demanded to be Lord of all my life as well. This created considerable tension within me because I knew that the way I was living was incompatible with what I felt God would want. I looked forward tremendously to the church meetings, but would rush out at the end in order to avoid getting known by Christians because I was guilty about many aspects of my lifestyle and wanted to cover them up. I wrongly anticipated that they would condemn me. One day, however, I was not quick enough, and was caught by David Pawson's secretary. Through her I was introduced to other people in the church and made friends, but in many ways this only increased the tension within me.

Eventually the pressure became too great and I reached a crisis point. For the second time in my life I knelt on the floor and asked God to do something. I wanted him to be the Lord of my life and was prepared to do whatever was necessary to make that a reality. I broke off the longstanding relationship, whose nature seemed at odds with the life I wanted to lead and which I felt would continue to drive a wedge between me and the God I wanted to get to know, and moved out of my flat to share with some other Christian girls and became involved with the church. From then on I knew that God had His hand firmly on my life and was working out His purposes in me.

The inner turmoil and sense of rejection that I had felt as a result of my experiences as a child, my sudden admission into hospital for instance and the removal of the tumour and my loneliness at boarding school, lay dormant for a while, as I involved myself in the life of the church, and slowly but surely began to take a more active role. Gradually the Lord brought these hurts and wounds into the open, and as they came to light, healed them and enabled me to receive the love, acceptance and forgiveness of Christ.

The process of healing was a long one. It began many years ago through the loving ministry of Mary Jones, a member of the ministry team of the church, and someone who was to become a very close and dear friend. She was the first person to tell me that not only did she have faith for my healing but also recognised God's calling and destiny on my life. She believed very strongly that I would be able to fulfil that calling, in spite of the emotional trauma I had suffered. It was through her that much of the healing work in my life was initiated.

The first time that I spoke to her about my difficulties with my eye as a child was both painful and full of hope. As I sat down with her and the group of people who were there to pray for me, she asked if there was anything I particularly wanted to talk about. As much as I wanted to let everything pour out, the words just would not come. My feelings were trapped behind an emotional dam, and it would take a lot to breach it. Mary waited patiently and gently encouraged me. As I began to explain how I felt about my experiences, the long buried feelings began to pour out in waves. The pain was so intense that I could barely speak. Mary waited as the tears came, allowing me simply to express my innermost feelings.

What happened next was quite unusual for Mary. She came to me, gathering everyone around to pray. There was nothing different about that, but as she began to pray it changed to prophecy. Mary told me that God had given me the gift of a second sight, as well as spiritual understanding, a special perception that not everyone possessed. My one remaining good eye was a mark of what God had done by His grace, and not only would He redeem, restore and heal me, but He would also take me further and enable me to use the gift of this perception to serve Him. Those were the first words I had ever heard which filled me with faith and hope for the future.

So began a long journey, one that would be costly at times, painful at others, but thoroughly rewarding. Little did I realise just what would be involved fulfilling my destiny when I heard those words. I had no idea of the obstacles I would have to overcome, the battles I would have to face, and the misunderstanding that would arise as a result of wishing to be faithful to the call of God on my life. Sometimes naivety is not such a bad thing! I was aware, however, that

God was prepared to take hold of a life like mine. I may not have been the best material in man's eyes, feeling emotionally battered and bruised, but the Lord saw the potential and began his healing work, slowly but surely opening up avenues of service and a life of fruitfulness.

2: By Default Or Design

From the very beginning of my ministry I realised that certain passages of Scripture appeared to debar women from church leadership. I knew that if I was to walk with integrity and maintain a clear conscience before God I would have to resolve this credibility gap. John says, 'Dear friends, if our hearts do not condemn us, we have confidence before God' (1 John 3.21). I realised that to work as a woman in a male dominated church, where prejudicial attitudes and sex roles are rigidly defined, I needed a secure understanding of the will of God for myself. I always had two main questions, 'am I hearing the voice of God?', and 'is my understanding scriptural?'.

As I submitted more of my life to the lordship of Jesus, and allowed Him to touch and heal the pain, I became more confident in myself. Slowly my ability to trust people grew and friendships deepened. Having realised how much the Lord had forgiven me, this motivated a strong zeal to serve Him. I was determined not to waste the life the Lord had given me and my desire to work for Him intensified as the months went by. After two years acquiring a good foundation of biblical teaching, I decided it was time to move on from Guildford. I believed I could more fruitfully use my teaching ability in needy countries of the world and with the backing of David Pawson, then the leader of Guildford Baptist Church, I applied to a mission to work in Addis Ababa. I was accepted and went to London to meet the mission directors for the final signing of contracts. My interview proceeded without problems until I was asked whether I believed in the baptism of the Holy Spirit. I replied that I did, because not to do so would be denying my experience. From that moment entry into that particular mission was closed because they did not share my belief. I felt disappointed, let down, even stunned. I remember walking out into the warm sunshine and wondering why this had happened. All I wanted to do was to serve God and it seemed the opportunity was being denied me. I went home with many questions buzzing around in my head, 'What could I do?', 'Where could I go?'. The only place to go was to God, so I prayed for His guidance and believed I would be shown the path He wanted me to tread.

Slowly the conviction that I should move away from Guildford faded. Within weeks I was asked to take a leadership role in the young people's work and I had a deep peace that this was the right course to take. It proved to be the beginning of a calling to leadership. I became involved in a whole variety of activities, especially developing artistic expressions in the church such as movement, drama and creative worship. I was often asked to help lead worship and participate in Sunday meetings. I chaired a group responsible for producing an Arts Festival to demonstrate crafts such as glass-blowing, macramé and lace-making, together with painting exhibitions, short performances of drama and many other artistic displays.

At one point I wrote and produced a large scale musical drama called '*Children of the King*' which involved a wide cross-section of the church. As I produced the play, I caught a glimpse of some of the difficulties I would face in the future. Whilst it was acknowledged that I had written the work and was perfectly capable of seeing it through, it was also felt that it was not right for a woman to be in overall charge, and a man was therefore, appointed as director over me. Fortunately the man appointed to the task was a friend and we worked well together.

By this time people had begun to trust me sufficiently to share their problems and I became increasingly involved in the pastoral side of the church, counselling and advising individuals and groups. I worked with colleagues on a variety of projects including a Guildford based pastoral group for those who had suffered loss called, '*A New Beginning*' and another group exploring the difficulties of being single. I also pioneered and devised a new concept of Christian teaching for use in our church for children up to the age of fifteen. I represented my church on numerous Christian committees in the town and learnt to work alongside people from many other denominations and persuasions. I enjoyed meeting others with different views and found these times stimulating, sometimes challenging, and very fulfilling.

With increasing responsibilities, time was at a premium. I became aware that to fulfil God's call on my life I would need more time to be able to develop further. I discussed this with a number of my close friends and colleagues and eventually decided that I would have to resign as a teacher and give myself full-time to the work I felt God was asking me to do. No-one made the decision for me. I had to act on what I believed was the right step to take. At that time there was no guarantee that the church would ask me onto its ministry team, and it was, therefore, a step of faith, even if it was with the encouragement of those closest to me.

I had financial commitments to meet, including a mortgage, but the day after I handed in my notice, God encouraged me with a letter from someone who knew nothing about what I was doing, in which she said: 'Brenda, God knows your need, do not be afraid or worry what you will eat or drink; or about your body, what you will wear. If God clothes the grass of the field, which is here today and tomorrow is thrown into the fire, will He not much more clothe you?'. It was only a small thing, but a confirmation of what I believed God was asking me to do. I left work and about four months later was invited to serve on the ministry team of the church; moreover, God proved His faithfulness to me, as He met every one of my financial needs. Some gave me gifts of money or essential commodities, others provided practical help free of charge.

For a number of years I had already been involved busily in the youth work, and was also encouraged by Mary Jones to help other people who needed healing in the emotional and spiritual areas of their lives. This was time consuming but very fulfilling and was a period of learning, teaching, being healed, and helping others to find healing. It was not without problems, but because of it I was stretched, challenged and found the scope of my ministry enlarged and increasingly fruitful.

In the early eighties a number of us involved in ministry and leadership came to the same conclusion: it was time to move on and start a new work. Out of this decision, which was by no means an easy one because of the many relationships we had formed, Guildford Community Church was born.

The tide of popular opinion in what are now termed the 'new' churches, was opposed to women in leadership, and the leadership of such fellowships and churches was predominantly male. The 'House Churches', as they were called, were formed as a result of dissatisfaction within the rigid structures of established denominations. At first there was a desire to see the whole denominational system disappear altogether. The Body of Christ seemed to be split over minor doctrinal differences, in the same way that the Corinthian church had been split, with some members following different personalities, such as Paul or Cephas.

A call went out from the House Churches to return to a Bible based view of the church. Plurality of leadership was quickly initiated and doctrines such as authority and submission were examined closely. Some of the theories and practices of the 'new churches' were treated with caution, or even opposition by outside observers.

A strong theme running through these churches was the role of men and women. Many of the initiators of these new groups had a Brethren history, with its firm belief that 'leadership is male'. Probably partly influenced by this history, and partly as a reaction to the rise of radical feminism, but also believing it to be scriptural, great emphasis was laid on the need for submission to each other. In practice people began to acknowledge gifts in each other and to submit to those who were clearly more gifted in certain areas than they were. This also meant that people were expected to submit to leaders in most matters, a practice heavily criticised outside the burgeoning movement and not completely without justification, since there were occasional abuses of this scriptural injunction.

The doctrine laid particular emphasis on the need for women to submit to their husbands. It was felt that, through the pronouncements of the feminist movements, the scriptural norm had been challenged and that families were suffering as a result. To be 'just' a home-maker was no longer considered an honourable career and the House Churches wanted to restore dignity to women who prepared a home for their families. In order for there to be structure in the home, however, certain scriptural principles had to be followed, one of which was the submission of wives to their husbands.

No one would argue that this principle is not mentioned in Scripture, but at times, it seems to me there is a tendency for a wife's submission to result in domination by the husband, who can easily forget his side of the deal i.e. to love his wife as Christ loved the church. More subtle than this, but certainly more far-reaching, was the principle in a number of churches of pursuing this out of the context of marriage. Carried to its logical conclusion the implication was that all women should submit to all men. I doubt if many would admit to it now, but this policy was pursued for a number of years. The result was, of course, that women stood no chance of being admitted into positions of leadership. How could they, if a man had a right to overrule them at any time?

The House Churches claimed to be returning to the biblical norm. They were careful to point out, however, that they were not reverting to a rigidly fundamentalist viewpoint. Many fundamentalists in fact had problems with much of House Church policy. As far as the role of women was concerned, however, nothing had changed. Ironically instead of the true biblical norm, their roles were even more clearly defined with less opportunity to express their God given gifts. They knew their 'God appointed' place and stayed there because they wanted to be obedient to the scriptures.

Guildford Community Church certainly fell into the category of a new church, and it was, therefore, not surprising that the issue of women should be raised right from the start.

The majority of people in our church believed that, because of their gifting, calling and obvious ability, three people should be given the responsibility of leading the group, namely Philip Vogel, Terry Brewer and myself. There was one small problem: I was a woman! Although they recognised my abilities to do the job, we were brought into terrible conflict because of the traditionally accepted biblical understanding of the role of women. A decision had to be made about whether

I was to be in leadership by man's default or God's design. Was I there simply because there was no man available to do the job, or because God had called me to that ministry?

The debate and discussion continued for some while. Early on one or two resigned from the church altogether and others threatened to; some remained with a certain amount of unease and wondered whether God could bless a church that appeared to be 'unscripturally' based; some wondered whether the weight of responsibility would be too much for me and questioned my strength to lead a church and others even asked whether I would be qualified to understand the problems of men. Sometimes Bible passages were cited as to why I was unsuitable and one person suggested that my motivation for wanting to lead was in itself a deception and therefore evil.

I must confess that at times I felt Scripture was being used as an excuse for prejudice rather than being viewed with an open mind in its proper context, but throughout it all I was affirmed by my two colleagues, Terry and Phil, as a church leader. Slowly others, when they saw the fruit of my ministry came round to this opinion and confirmed their support for me. Men and women alike told me that although they had difficulties with the idea of women in leadership, there was little doubt in their minds that God had anointed me for this task.

Not everyone in the church agreed immediately with what I was doing, and I had to learn to be secure, not only in my calling as a Christian, but also in my calling to be a leader. For about three years, as people worked through the difficulties they had with my role, it was important for me to listen to their misgivings and dilemmas and so help them find answers for themselves to the questions they faced.

As much as I wanted people to express their feelings, it was a very difficult time for me, and I needed a lot of support when my life seemed to be under constant scrutiny. I found it hard not to take people's genuine questions about the role of women as a personal attack. I survived, however, and know that during this period I developed a far greater trust in the Lord. I came to the conclusion that if God was calling me to be a leader, then others, provided they had an open mind on the subject, would accept that 'by their fruits you will recognise them' (Matthew 7.16).

I approached my leadership role a little tentatively at first, because of my own and other uncertainties, but as time went by I grew in confidence and assumed more responsibility. Initially I was in charge of much of the pastoral care of the church, but also played a significant part in any decision making. The establishment of the leadership team, and especially my role in it, was a long and painful operation during which time I seriously doubted my own ability to do the job. There was formidable opposition too, notably from one particular individual who wielded considerable influence at that time. Whenever I counselled or prayed for people, he would suggest, in a very negative way, that women should not be doing that kind of job. He went so far as to hint that I was using the power of the evil one to help people. Because of this my leadership was gradually undermined and after many months I felt badly shaken and concerned about my future role in the church.

Around the same period I attended an inter-church leaders evening. The guest speaker was Ian Andrews, who explained the strategies of our spiritual enemies. When he had finished speaking, he began to minister to a number of people, with words of knowledge from the Holy Spirit for their particular situation. He felt that almost every one of them needed deliverance of some kind, and together we prayed and set people free from the oppression of the enemy. Then he turned to me and said, 'You do not need deliverance, but you need to know that you are anointed by God.'

Tears of relief flowed down my face. My calling had been tested in no uncertain terms but here was God confirming it independently. I realised that if our spiritual enemies cannot prevent a work beginning, they will mount a concerted campaign to stop it being established. This tactic seemed to have been used on me but God, in his mercy, stepped in at the right time to thwart the enemy's plans.

I woke in the early hours of the following morning knowing beyond a shadow of doubt that God had called me to lead, and secure in the knowledge that He had given me the ability to do so. I no longer felt that I had to prove myself to anyone, and was freed from having to hold a particular position, or to fight for it. I experienced the reality of the fact that the battle is not mine but the Lord's.

I had begun to feel much more comfortable with my leadership role, but a few nagging questions remained, the main ones being . . .

1. *Was my leadership role compatible with the Scriptures?* Without the assurance that I was in line with the word of God I could not continue in my present role. Biblical confirmation was essential if I was to remain in leadership.

2. *Are women more easily deceived than men?* Had Eve set a precedent in the Garden of Eden which meant that all women after her would be as easily deceived? I had to face this possibility and be clear in my own mind as to its validity in order to lead with confidence and be free from the fear of falling into the same trap.

3. *Do women have an inbuilt inferiority and weakness which renders them unable to govern?* This accusation often

levelled at women to explain their unsuitability for leadership needed to be looked at more closely to determine its legitimacy.

4. *Why did Jesus not choose both men and women to be among his original group of disciples?* The argument that all Jesus' disciples were male is frequently used as a basis to exclude women from a place at Jesus' side in leadership. I needed to discover whether this was a good enough reason for making leadership a male domain.

Naturally I automatically turned to the scriptures to answer those questions besides reading other books and documents. I also listened to other people on the subject and through it all attempted to hear the inner witness of my own heart.

The answers that silenced my questions may not satisfy yours. Each of us needs to be convinced in our own minds, and find answers from the Scriptures for ourselves. This does not preclude, however, the need for an adequate doctrinal basis for our actions and beliefs. There were certain keys which resolved my own areas of doubt, and I have set these out in the following pages. It is not intended to be a critical interpretation of Scripture.

1. Was my leadership role compatible with the Scriptures?

I realised that commonly held interpretations of the scriptural role of men and women were not as clear cut as I had previously been led to believe. The author and speaker Gerald Coates demonstrated how easy it is to misuse Scripture in this sort of context when commenting on 'the place and role of women'. He likened the issue of women in leadership in the Church to the abolition of the slave trade, mentioning the tremendous role that William Wilberforce played and the amount of opposition that he experienced. Sadly most of the opposition was from the Church. Wilberforce was told that since the Bible clearly taught that slaves should be subject to their masters, there must be a place for slaves in society! Such logic would lead us to believe that for no other reason, women cannot be in leadership because Scripture teaches that an elder should be: 'the husband of but one wife' (1 Timothy 3.2). How could this possibly apply to women? Incredible as it may seem, I have heard this argument used!

My study brought me to a fresh realization that the Bible must be understood in its cultural context. A friend of mine once said, 'If all the commands of the Scriptures are to be taken literally, why do we not wash each other's feet more often?!' Jesus did not intend that we should perpetuate the action of washing feet for all time, but that we should apply the spirit of His instruction to different areas of our lives.

I did not want to look at isolated passages of Scripture alone, but tried to see the text as a whole. Out of context a text is in danger of becoming a pretext. If I wanted answers to my questions, therefore, I needed to look further that individual passages, to try and see threads and themes running throughout the Bible. I realised also that interpretation of the Scriptures must take into account the context in which each particular part was written, the authors, the historical background and a whole host of other factors.

I looked at passages that have been frequently quoted and analysed in the debate about the role of women, since it was crucial for me to have a clear understanding of these portions of Scripture. Many others have researched them in far greater depth and a bibliography appears at the end of the book for further reading. What I would like to convey here are my thoughts on these particular passages, and what I feel God revealed to me through them:

'Now I want you to realise that the head of every man is Christ, and the head of the woman is man, and the head of Christ is God. Every man who prays or prophesies with his head covered dishonours his head. And every woman who prays or prophesies with her head uncovered dishonours her head – it is just as though her head were shaved. If a woman does not cover her head, she should have her hair cut off; and if it is a disgrace for a woman to have her hair cut or shaved off, she should cover her head.' (1 Corinthians 11. 3–16).

The government of the day was Roman and legally a man was the absolute head of his household. His wife and children were his property and they had no rights of their own. A husband held the power of life and death over his spouse and he may even have been expected to divorce her if she appeared improperly dressed in public. By removing her head covering in public and exposing her hair, she was announcing to the world her sexual promiscuity and dubious moral character. Full loose hair was a sex symbol in the minds of Jewish women, as well as the Corinthian gentile converts. In his booklet 'The New Humanity', Roger Forster, leader of the Icthus Fellowship in South East London writes, 'Jewish women attending the love feast would wear a veil or hair symbol which indicated that they were married. Jewish women tied their hair up on their wedding day and were never seen otherwise in public without their wedding symbol.'

It seemed reasonable to me to conclude that Paul, whilst encouraging freedom, was also suggesting that women should be circumspect and conform to culturally accepted standards. The Corinthian church became embroiled in the very same immorality for which Corinth was renowned and it seemed to me that Paul was ensuring that every step was taken to avoid further misunderstanding. Only a loose woman would appear in public without a veil. The head covering was a sign of a woman's propriety. When he writes, 'Judge for yourselves: is it proper for a woman to pray to God with her head uncovered?' (1 Corinthians 11.13), I believe he is asking us to decide what is correct behaviour for ourselves in the light of its cultural appropriateness. Perhaps he asks the question because he is wise enough to realise that the answer may be different in cultures other than those with which he is familiar, and thus he is encouraging us to think and act rationally and responsibly in our own situation.

Having established that the wearing of a veil is cultural, I came to realise, through studying commentators views on these verses, that a veil is not necessarily a sign of submission. The word that is translated veil in 1 Corinthians 11 verse 10 in some versions, is replaced by 'a sign of authority' in the New International Version. This is because it is literally taken from the word *exousia* and means freedom of action or the right to act. It is the same word used of God and includes the concept of being absolutely free and unrestricted. It is a symbol of authority. Paul is saying that a woman ought to have the freedom to pray, prophesy and play a full part in church life.

'Now I want you to realise that the head of every man is Christ, and the head of the woman is man, and the head of Christ is God' (1 Corinthians 11.3). If Paul was introducing the concept of hierarchy, he surely would have begun with . . . 'the head of Christ is God'. He does not, however, and I found myself wondering exactly what Paul was trying to convey. Matthew Henry, in his own inimitable way conveys something of what I believe was God's intention and Paul's understanding: 'The woman was made of a rib out of the side of Adam; not made out of his head to top him, not made out of his feet to be trampled on by him, but out of his side to be equal with him, under his arm to be protected, and near his heart to be loved.'

The word 'head' translated here in this Corinthian passage can equally be rendered as 'source' as in the source of a river. Just as Adam was created unique by the Lord God, so was Eve. Paul underlines this point when he writes, 'In the Lord, however, woman is not independent of man, nor is man independent of woman. For as woman came from man, so also man is born of woman. But everything comes from God' (1 Corinthians 11.11). All are equal before Christ in this new order.

Paul was not seeking to introduce hierarchy or to minimise freedom. His concern was to underline freedom without causing unnecessary offence to unbelievers present when the church came together. His priority was to glorify God in our behaviour.

'. . . women should remain silent in the churches. They are not allowed to speak, but must be in submission, as the Law says. If they want to inquire about something, they should ask their husbands at home; for it is disgraceful for a woman to speak in the church.' (1 Corinthians 14.34–35).

If this passage prohibits any woman speaking in a church meeting at any time, or suggests that men should not submit to women, it would contradict other parts of the New Testament. The majority of Jewish women in Paul's day would not have been educated in the same way as the men. They were not used to the idea of learning and being taught that many of the new converts were suddenly enjoying. It is likely that, in their new found freedom, they were becoming over enthusiastic, and perhaps even abusing that freedom.

The word that is here translated as 'speak' might be better translated as 'chatter' or 'babble'. Paul is addressing the problem of unruly church meetings and is saying that disorder is created by people chattering and interrupting with questions. It is also likely that the phrase 'silent under certain conditions' is a truer reflection of 'keep quiet' in verse 28 and 'remain silent' in verse

34. Again this would seem to be substantiated by the fact that Paul is looking for a way to solve the problem of disorder in the meetings.

'I want men everywhere to lift up holy hands in prayer, without anger or disputing. I also want women to dress modestly, with decency and propriety, not with braided hair or gold or pearls or expensive clothes, but with good deeds, appropriate for the women who profess to worship God.

A woman should learn in quietness and full submission. I do not permit a woman to teach or to have authority over a man; she must be silent. For Adam was formed first, then Eve. And Adam was not the one deceived; it was the woman who was deceived and became a sinner. But women will be kept safe through childbirth, if they continue in faith, love and holiness with propriety' (1 Timothy 2.8–15).

The emphasis in this passage so often overlooked is that 'A woman should learn'. As we have already seen, that was a revolutionary concept for the woman of that time. Although verse twelve is usually translated 'I do not permit a woman to teach or have authority over a man, she must be silent', the verb used is in the present tense and should in fact read, 'I am not presently permitting . . .'

It would seem to be sensible that someone who had only just started to learn, should not be given authority to teach the whole congregation. Paul did not regard this as an all time command; how could he when later we read that a woman was outstanding among the apostles. Roman 16 verse 7 talks of Junius, one of Paul's relatives who became a Christian before him. The majority of commentators agree that there is strong evidence that Junius was a woman.

Contrary to current popular opinion, Paul was actually making radical statements which would be hard for men to swallow. 'Let a woman learn' was an all-time command that the men of the time would not have found easy to accept, any more than the men of today find it easy to let women preach. Far from my leadership role not being compatible with Scripture, I have discovered the reverse to be true. Paul's words are largely quoted out of context and it is probable that he was more concerned with wider issues of doctrine and behaviour than in subjugating women. Paul seems to me in fact to underline a woman's freedom to minister and to fulfil everything God has in mind for her.

2. Are women more easily deceived than men?

Until I had faced and answered this question, my confidence was easily undermined. How could I be sure that my opinions were right if I differed from my male colleagues on an issue. I had difficulty in sticking with my convictions, no doubt subconsciously thinking 'they are more likely to be right, I must be deceived'. With this type of uncertainty lurking beneath the surface, I found myself over-compensating by expressing my opinions far more dogmatically than was necessary.

Through their reading of Genesis chapter 3, and the passage in 1 Timothy 2 verses 6–15, where it clearly states that Eve was the one 'who was deceived', many have concluded that all women have an inbuilt weakness and are more vulnerable to deception than men. They should not, therefore, be allowed to teach and hold positions of authority. This cannot be supported, however, since neither Scripture nor history substantiates this view. Can one woman's deception be seen as a reason for denying all subsequent generations positions of responsibility? God appointed women to positions of authority and they were capable of commanding respect as leaders. Some notable examples in the Bible include:

Huldah – a well known prophetess, respected to the extent that her advice was sought by the King of Judah (2 Kings 22.14–20).

Deborah – another prophetess who, the scriptures tell us, was leading Israel. She judged all the disputes among the people, and was obviously a woman of some renown and courage. Barak was certainly not very happy about going into battle without her, even if it meant that hers would be the honour for winning the fight. Perhaps the most significant phrase used about Deborah's time as a leader in Israel is 'The land had peace for forty years' (Judges chapters 4 and 5).

The New Testament describes *Pheobe* in Romans 16 verse 1 as '. . . a servant of the church in Cenchrea'. The word servant here means deacon/diakonos, a masculine term used by Paul about himself and other men. There are no grounds to suppose that her role was any different from that of other male deacons or ministers.

Acts 18 verse 26 tells us that *Priscilla* taught Apollos, and despite currently held views that women should not teach men, there is no indication that this was regarded as unseemly, unusual or strange by Apollos.

Philippians 4 verse 2 mentions two women, *Euodia* and *Syntyche* as leaders of the church in Philippi. Paul praises these women in glowing terms for their efforts for the gospel and refers to them as his fellow-workers. Unfortunately these two were apparently not getting along too well and Paul has to confront them. They were obviously in such prominent positions in the church that their personal quarrels were a threat to its harmonious life. That does not distract from the fact, however, that Paul did not regard it as strange for them to be in leadership, nor did he call them to stand down.

The history of Christianity shows women to be fierce defenders and fearless proclaimers of the truth. Amongst them are those who have brought about much needed social reform, and taken a strong lead both at home and overseas in fighting injustice and evil.

Mary Slessor served in West Africa for thirty-nine years, gaining great influence with the indigenous population, and helping to bring to an end many kinds of cruelty. In 1905, the British Government officially recognised her authority and invested in her the powers of a magistrate, which she exercised until her death in 1915.

Elizabeth Fry (1780–1845), despite having a large family herself, taught poor, uneducated children and preached regularly as an 'approved minister' in Quaker gatherings. She is probably best remembered for initiating the improvement in conditions for female prisoners. Her work began in Newgate Prison, but was eventually to influence prisons throughout England and beyond.

Gladys Aylward's endeavours to spread the gospel in China's remote Yangcheng region were strengthened when she was appointed foot inspector by the local Mandarin. This was to enforce the new law prohibiting the ancient and crippling custom of female foot-binding. She took advantage of her position and contacts to preach the gospel. She is probably remembered best for the epic journey she made leading a hundred children to safety during the Japanese invasion of 1940.

Together *William* and *Catherine Booth* established the Salvation Army. Catherine preached regularly and became a famous orator. The Booth's seventh child, Evangeline, eventually took over the command of the Salvation Army in the United States.

In 1973, the Yugoslav born *Mother Teresa* became the first *woman* to win the Templeton Prize for Religion. This annual award is given to 'stimulate the knowledge and love of God on the part of mankind everywhere'. All the £34,000 prize money was given by Mother Teresa to the order she had founded, *The Sisters of Charity*. This was initially established to help the poor and dying of Calcutta. Today Mother Teresa has initiated similar works around the world, run by people from many different denominations.

History has revealed that, far from being unable to lead, many women have proved the reverse to be true. Instead of being deceived, they have boldly proclaimed truth, exposing social evils, penetrating the darkness of many people's lives with the unchanging gospel of Jesus, and bringing about radical reform both on a personal and social level.

God has clearly called and equipped his female servants to lead. They have almost always found an avenue for service, despite restrictions placed upon them by the Church, which not only revealed their determination to carry out the task to which they felt God had called them, but also, I believe, indicated God's desire for them to be free to fulfil their potential in exactly the same way as men.

I am always puzzled by the fact that if women are so vulnerable to deception, and therefore untrustworthy where 'real' responsibility in the Church is concerned, God the Father felt perfectly happy to entrust His son Jesus to a woman. She was called to conceive and bear the Saviour of the world. God clearly considered her adequate for this awesome task.

In Jewish society, naming a person is a sign of authority. Jesus, for example, had the authority to change Simon's name to Peter. When Adam first saw the woman God had made for him, he said, 'She shall be called woman (she-man)', which means that he noticed the difference in her sexuality, but did not give her a name at this point. The Hebrew verb 'to call' usually only infers an establishment of authority when it is linked with the noun 'name'. In Genesis 2 verse 23 that particular noun is absent. There is no official naming by Adam of his helper until after the fall when he calls her *Eve*. Only then is his dominance asserted over her and a pattern formed which would be adopted in Jewish society for centuries to come.

When the angel Gabriel appeared to *Mary* to tell her the momentous news that she would conceive a son through the Holy Spirit, he said: 'You will be with child and give birth to a son and you are to give him the name Jesus.' (Luke 1.31). Significantly this act of naming her son included the verb and noun together, indicating that Mary had been given the authority to name Jesus.

That Jesus entrusted the message of His resurrection to women cannot be under-estimated. The risen Christ first appeared to *Mary Magdalene* and gave her the responsibility of carrying the good news to his disciples who were still in hiding, fearful and uncertain of the future. All the gospel writers considered this significant enough to record. I believe there is a parallel between the garden of Eden and the garden of Resurrection. In the second garden, Christ demonstrates to all who would follow him that women need no longer be overshadowed by the consequences of Eve's deception.

In Jewish society, men laid the bulk of responsibility for the Fall upon women. It is clear from Genesis chapter 3, however, that God considers them both culpable. If only one was responsible he would not have punished them both. Paul the apostle also refutes this argument by saying that Adam was equally responsible for the Fall (Romans 5. 12ff).

Eve was deceived it is true, but Adam was gullible and disobedient. Adam's sin didn't necessarily give all men after him an inbuilt propensity to gullibility, why then should Eve's sin also be transferred specifically to all women? If we are to draw conclusions from the Garden of Eden, rather than singling out Eve as some are prone to do, let us look at the part both played in the sin. Each was culpable, each sinned in different ways but as Christians we have been cleansed by the blood of Jesus who came to redeem us from the sin.

3. Do women have an inbuilt inferiority and weakness which renders them unable to govern?

It is often argued that because woman was created after man, she is inferior to him. If that line of argument is pursued human beings are inferior to the animals! Paul writes concerning physical strength: 'Husbands, in the same way be considerate as you live with your wives, and treat them with respect as the weaker partner . . .' (1 Peter 3.7). The word weaker here in the Greek is 'asthenesteros', which means 'of less physical strength'. Obviously, in this sense women are, on the whole, the weaker sex. This verse seems to have been misapplied, however, and used for other concepts of strength, including logic and objectivity, traditionally male domains. That women are assumed not to possess these qualities has rendered them by men as emotionally weak.

These attributes have of course nothing to do with emotional strength, and there is no reason to suppose that women are weaker in any other sense than physical. My research has shown me that in both history and the Bible, women have demonstrated their ability and competence to govern and have been given the qualities by God to do so.

4. Why did Jesus not choose both men and women to be among his original group of disciples?

John Noble, one of the foremost leaders of the House Church movement or New Churches as they are now called, addressed this question with the following comment: 'That Jesus appointed twelve male disciples is obvious and they were also Jews. Simply because all the disciples were male, however, does not mean there should be no female disciples any more than all disciples of Jesus must be Jews.'

Jesus was never exclusive. We know only too well that he intended both Gentiles and Jews to belong to the church and that many of those Gentile converts would eventually become church leaders. Equally, the fact that the initial inner circle of twelve disciples was only men is no foundation on which to base an assumption that Jesus never intended women to be his followers, or indeed to hold positions of responsibility.

Jesus behaved radically in His treatment of women, particularly since He was respected as a Rabbi of some note. He continually set new precedents in treating them with dignity and counted them among his closest friends. Some of his relationships with women could even be likened to that of a Rabbi to his disciples. We see this so clearly when Mary sits at the feet of Jesus, eagerly drinking in all that he had to say, being encouraged by Jesus to continue doing so (Luke 10. 38–41).

To the woman at the well in Samaria Jesus first revealed he was the Messiah (John 4.26). Far from being considered inferior to men, Jesus treated women as equals, spending time preparing them for ministry which He believed they were quite capable of carrying out.

Over a long period of time, my questions were answered. The research and study took several years, and my conclusions outlined above were the result of much study and heart searching. Gradually the dilemmas were resolved as I discovered that the life of Jesus supported my conclusions. It had been crucial for me to know that the pathway I was pursuing in leadership was Godly and scriptural. As this was confirmed to me, the result was peace within myself and confidence to continue along the road I believed God had called me.

My personal conclusions did not necessarily convince everyone immediately, and there were still struggles to be faced. Even today I received letters addressed to Bryn

Robson or Brendon Robson, so sure are the writers that the leader of Guildford Community Church must be a man. Some people outside our church still refuse to write to me if they want information about our activities and insist on writing to a male member of the team. But, Rome wasn't built in a day, and centuries of teaching cannot be dispelled in a few short years.

3: Against The Odds

Resolving a number of theological questions was a key to unlocking some of the emotional dilemmas: '. . . be transformed by the renewing of your mind' (Romans 12.26). However much this helped, an historical legacy of emotional disqualification, which has profoundly affected modern women, still had to be overcome. Confession of emotional pain and insecurities is essential for wholeness as God intended. I struggled to know how best to do this, however, without that very disclosure, giving the impression that I was emotionally unstable, and thereby confirming the myth of feminine unreliability and inferiority. This seemed to my inevitable catch 22.

Throughout history women have been branded as emotionally orientated creatures who cannot think rationally, logically and objectively and are therefore incapable of leading. They have inherited a legacy, by virtue of their so-called sensitive natures, which I will call emotional disqualification. Many women I have met feel that this disqualification has served as a barrier to their involvement in meaningful leadership roles. They find they are included in a leadership forum for some aspects of the work, but as soon as church strategy appears on the agenda, they are excluded.

I know a woman who was a member of the leadership team in her church, and during a difficult phase in its development, the team invited another man to come and give them advice. The initial meeting took place in the home of the couple who both happened to be leaders. When the gentleman who had been invited in to help saw the woman, however, he said, 'This is not for you, I will only speak to men.' Although she was a full member of the team, and the meeting was taking place in her home, she was requested and strongly encouraged by the rest of the team, including her husband, to be obedient and sit in the kitchen whilst the men discussed what should happen to the church. This is not an isolated occurrence.

Another woman told me that she was regarded as a person who 'feels', which implied that she could not think things through logically, but relied totally on her intuition. It was considered impossible to build anything in the church on something as variable and unreliable as feelings. Her own giftings and abilities were therefore regarded with suspicion. She could only attend leadership meetings when she had something specific to say. When she was allowed to attend meetings, and her perspective proved right and reliable in almost every case, the men still could not accept her formally into their leadership group. They seemed unable to acknowledge publicly that she had a legitimate contribution to make, perhaps because they could not cope with her 'strength of feelings'.

At the opening meeting of a large conference, the five main speakers were introduced, one of them a woman. All were asked to introduce themselves briefly and say what they would be speaking about during the conference. After the woman had spoken, the last man to be introduced moved to the microphone and said, 'If this woman is going to speak at this conference, then I will not!' The humiliation and emotional damage caused by incidents like this is easy to imagine, and it is hardly surprising that some women give up trying to be accepted as equal partners altogether. Cornered, not knowing how to solve the problem, they feel caught between confessing their struggles, and knowing that this may be viewed as the very reason for their exclusion.

The subjugation of women was foretold by God: 'Your desire will be for your husband and he will rule over you' (Genesis 3.16). The suppression of women has been built into the foundations of almost every society throughout the world. In many cultures women belong to their husbands, to be used as they wished, and when considered no longer useful discarded and left destitute. Such was the case even in Jesus' day, when a husband could divorce his wife on a whim leaving her with no financial or material security, and with no alternative but to turn to prostitution. Women were regarded as on a par with animals and other unclean things. The Jewish classic, the Talmud, mirrors the life and thought of the communities in Palestine from around 200 B.C. to 500 A.D. and makes a number of comments about women:

'A man is obliged to offer three benedictions daily, that He has made me Israelite, that He has not made me a woman, and that He has not made me a boor' (Men 43b).

'Ten measures of speech descended to the world, women took nine and men one' (Kid 49b).

'Women are light minded' (Shab 33b).

'It is the way of women to remain at home, and for man to go into the market place and learn intelligence from other men' (Gen.R. 18 v 1).

'Women are addicted to witchcraft' (Joma 8 v 3b).

The Talmud offers clear guidance as to the selection of a wife, which rather suggests that women had to fulfil particular qualifications and men had free choice in the matter. Daughters had no choice at all because marriages were arranged by their fathers.

There is much in Christian practise that has preserved the church from this kind of extreme thought and behaviour. The commands to love one another, care for one another, honour and prefer one another, are directives that are applicable to all people everywhere, regardless of sex. They are basic groundrules that to some extent have saved women from many of the excesses to be found in other religions and philosophies of the world.

A huge mosque stands in the East End of London, dominating the landscape. All mosques have a separate entrance for women, and this is no exception. The door for the men is at the front of the building, and that for the women on the side. Over the side entrance are the words 'Women, animals and other unclean things'.

A cursory glance at Taoist philosophy reveals its view of women. Taoism taught that the entire universe was formed by, and comprises, balanced yet opposing forces known as 'yin' and 'yand'. Yin represents the negative forces such as evil, darkness, coldness, the moon and femaleness, while Yang represents the positive forces such as good, light, heat, sun and maleness.

Christianity has created groundrules that prevent too much abuse. It gives honour and value to people generally. While it is true that most Christian men honour and value women for themselves, often that respect is patronising, and if a woman steps outside of clearly defined areas and starts to push down a few barriers, the respect evaporates and their value seems to vanish with it.

The accusation is often levelled against those who are attempting to shed light on the issue of women in the church, that they have been seduced by the feminist argument. In fact a closer look at the life of the Church, and the attitudes to be found within it, would show that the Church itself has absorbed the values of the world on this matter, in its continued suppression of women.

Jesus' example and message gave new hope to women, promising real potential and vision to revolutionise their situation. His achievement, however, was soon lost. Not so very long after his ascension, the traditional role and position of women in the home and society was to be rediscovered and firmly entrenched throughout Christian history.

By the close of the second century, Clement of Alexandria, while affirming that men and women were equal in the sight of God, laid down some clear guidelines as to acceptable behaviour from women. Their behaviour was to be quiet and modest, pure and chaste. I suppose no one could argue too much with that! But he went on to decree that God's plan for women was to 'spend their time, when not at prayer, in spinning, weaving, making and embroidering garments, the care of the household and the preparation of food'.

At about the same time the historian Tertullian wrote, 'The judgment of God upon your sex (women) endures even today and with it inevitably endures your position of criminal at the bar of justice. You are the gateway to the devil'.

Later writers in the third and fourth centuries, including Saint Gerome, pursued and developed this theme until extravagance in dress was deplored, together with cosmetics, and women were encouraged to spend much time in prayer and meditation. They were obviously not to be trusted in other areas of life!

Christianity was established in England in the fifth century when Saint Columba sailed from Ireland to the island of Iona to found the first British monastery and a Christian mission. With him came these attitudes towards women. By this time Christianity had lost its radical edge as far as women were concerned. They had already been put well and truly back in their place.

In Medieval and Norman England there were two main influences upon men and women: the Feudal system and the Church. The place into which each person was born in society was regarded as that which had been ordained by God and nothing could and should change that. Although British women had until then been entitled to hold land in their own right, this was soon to disappear and women were romanticised as gentle, untouchable beings. There was an unspoken assumption that a woman's one and only desire in life was to be whisked off by a knight in shining armour. Their place was ostensibly still in the home, producing heirs and serving their husband.

During the Reformation, Protestantism was established and eventually encompassed all those within the Christian tradition outside Roman Catholicism. The main theologians, Luther, Zwingli, Calvin and Knox, who broke away from the then Catholic Church, did much to bring new understanding to that unenlightened age. Their efforts, however, seemed to bring little relief to the plight of women. Indeed Luther said, 'I have taught you Christ, purely, simply and without adulteration', which he did. But he also said with regard to women, 'Never any good came out of female domination. God created Adam master and lord of living creatures, but Eve spoiled all'.

A paper entitled, '*The first blast of the trumpet against the monstrous regiment of women*', written by reformist theologian John Knox, said of women, 'Nature doth paint them to be weak, frail, impatient, feeble and foolish, and experience hath declared them to be inconstant, variable, cruel and lacking the spirit of counsel'.

By the 17th century, the Authorised version of the Bible was translated into English and found in virtually every village and many homes. For ordinary people it was the only book they knew. The reformed theological interpretation of the Scriptures, therefore, had a marked influence on belief. Even King James who had authorised the version did not seem to have been slow in expressing his views concerning the education of women. He said: 'To make women learned and foxes tamed hath the same effect . . . to make them cunning!'

Generally, during the Stuart and Commonwealth years, men did not like their women to be learned. It is fair to say that throughout the eighteenth, and well into the nineteenth century, the belief that woman was mentally inferior to man was constantly aired and believed by the majority of both sexes.

In the 1800s the first trade unions had been formed, but women were not welcomed into them for fear that they would tend to keep wages too low. For mid-Victorian girls brought up with the one aim of marriage, the only alternative was lonely spinsterhood, for there soon dawned the realisation that there were not enough eligible young men to go round. If a girl could not find a husband and her father was unable to leave her enough money for a private income – what was she to do? She could become a paid companion or enter teaching-the only profession open to her – and for which she had no solid learning or training, even if she possessed the aptitude. Work in a factory or shop was unthinkable for a middle-class girl, for she must, come what may, maintain her social status.

In Victorian England, although some changes were to take place, little seemed to challenge the view held by both sexes that women were inferior to men. Wives seemed to believe that their only true power lay in the ability to manipulate the minds and actions of their partners. I find frightening reflections of that view in many women today. How often have you heard, 'He may be the head of the family, but I am the neck that turns the head'? This implies quite clearly that if wives do not or cannot express their opinions openly to their husbands, they can make timely suggestions instead to make their partners see their point of view. In other words, subtle manipulation.

In the mid 19th century, land, children, personal belongings, even jewellery, as well as a woman's body were the property of her husband. Even the courts stated that a man could imprison his wife to 'restrain her from liberty for an indefinite time'. In short, a woman had no legal rights at all. It was still a husband's right to kidnap and imprison his wife until 1891 when for the first time a husband was convicted for unlawfully restraining his partner[1].

Until comparatively recently, the only way a woman of the 'comfortable classes' could achieve financial security and social status was to marry and consign herself solely to her husband. Not until some way through this century did married women own anything.

Media images become very important after World War 1 when women, having served faithfully in the munition factories, retreated to their homes. The image portrayed between the wars was of the comfortable middle-class woman, probably not representative of the majority, domestic service remaining the largest single area of female employment. Of the 2.7 million women employed, 2 million were in domestic service.

With the advent of the Second World War, 1914 repeated itself. Women were needed for the war effort and brought back to work. The image portrayed by the media was 'the woman behind the man behind the gun', but by the end of the war women had disappeared from the labour force once again.

Since that time, Acts of Parliament have been passed concerning equal pay and equal opportunities, designed to stop discrimination in the workplace and advertising against women. It is now even possible for a woman to get her husband turned out of her house if he beats or mistreats her and it is almost impossible for the husband to do the same.

---

[1] Criminal law, evidence and procedure, Vol 2 Sect 1214. Regina v Jackson

Before euphoria sets in, however, it would appear that since the Reformation, the traditional view that women could not hold positions of responsibility because of emotional inferiority and weakness has, with only a few exceptions, never been challenged. This would apply especially, but by no means exclusively, to the Church. Even today, the results of many different psychological tests have shown that masculinity is still valued more highly than femininity by both men and women. Some while ago friends shared this riddle with me: 'Mr Smith and his son were involved in a car accident in which Mr Smith died instantly. The son was rushed to the nearest hospital and whisked into the operating theatre for immediate surgery. The surgeon exclaimed, "I can't operate on him, he's my son!"' Explain why not, they asked me. I found my response interesting in that it took some time for me to realise the answer. Before reading on, can you explain the riddle? . . . The simple explanation is that the surgeon was the boy's mother! I suspect that the majority of us are unconsciously conditioned to believe that only men hold responsible positions. Ask most men what sex they would like their first child to be, and almost invariably it will be male. There still exists a cultural bias in our society which makes the assumption that men are superior and should, therefore, take precedence over women.

With such a weight of history against them, it is hardly surprising that women have struggled against this legacy of emotional disqualification. I count myself among them, but it became imperative for me to be set free from it, for I firmly believed that Jesus had come to set me free from all bondage, that the person whom the Son sets free, is free indeed, and: 'where the Spirit of the Lord is, there is freedom' (2 Corinthians 3.17).

Emotional freedom

Neither emotional awareness as individuals, nor public expression of our feelings have been encouraged in Britain. In fact, quite the reverse. Boys are brought up believing it is unmanly to cry. From a very early age we are taught that one does not make a fuss in public, despite there being very good reason for it. Even on the saddest occasions such as funerals, it is often regarded as unseemly to appear too moved or distraught. We are expected to remain fully in control of our feelings at all times, and as a result we grow up continually suppressing deep emotions and become inhibited as adults in this area of our lives. Generally speaking this applies less to girls than boys. In Britain we are still proud of our 'stiff upper lip'.

Many men and women are embarrassed to demonstrate expressions of love, affection or care outside of the marital context. In recent years, inside certain churches, men can be seen hugging men, and women embracing women, but never outside the safety of a church meeting. To do so would certainly raise a few eyebrows and even raise suspicions of homosexuality.

At my college in London we were told, 'You are some of the top five per cent of the country', and 'You are among the cream of our nation'. When I consider comments like that now I realise they helped to create a superior attitude among us and also reflected a generally held belief that intellect and results are more important than attitudes and feelings. What we believe affects our actions. The church has not escaped this outlook. I have heard it said, 'Women are "feelers" and nothing should be built on anything as irrational as that'. The facts, however, clearly show that there are many theorists among both men and women who struggle with their feelings. My own research into this matter has shown that the word 'mind' in the Scriptures incorporates feelings. *Vines Expository Dictionary of Words* says: 'The mind is the seat of reflective consciousness comprising the faculties of perception and understanding and those of *feeling*, judging and determining.'

Emotions are, therefore, an integral part of decision-making and judging processes. The precious gift of intuition is the harmony between our emotions and mind. If emotions disqualify us from holding positions of leadership, Jesus Himself should have been prohibited from carrying out his ministry. He wept in public a number of times over the hardness of men's hearts and their failure to see the truth. He grieved over the death of a friend. He was so indignant at one stage that He forcibly ejected people and objects from the Temple area.

We are made in His image. Feelings are a part of our created being and should not, therefore, disqualify us from carrying responsibility. On the contrary, we need them to help us understand situations and problems, and thus they are an integral part of authentic spirituality. They are involved in the very essence of judging and assessing and are, therefore, at the very heart of decision making including church government.

This realisation helped me to express my emotional and psychological struggles verbally. I was no longer so fearful of sharing my dilemmas with trustworthy friends, although I have to admit to wondering occasionally what their response would be. It involved becoming vulnerable, a risky business for a number of reasons, not least that people might not have understood and I could easily have lost my reputation for being able to cope. Men, of course, because of the emotional conditioning they have had to endure, would consider the latter point of far greater importance.

Being aware of our past and present feelings is important in understanding our weaknesses and limitations. Although personal history is no excuse for the sin we commit, it is important to know the reasons behind our behaviour. We often over-react to present situations because we are responding from unresolved issues from the past. If we have hidden grief for example, or come from a home where there was a great deal of anger, or were the brother or sister of a child who was always preferred by our parents, then we will react when similar situations confront us in adult life.

We need not only God's grace for today, but also His healing and freedom from traumas still troubling us from the past. If we do not allow God to touch these areas, they remain weaknesses which can be exploited and over which we have little or no control. God is able to resolve my questions of the past because He is not limited by time and space. He is not only God of today and tomorrow, but also of yesterday.

I had always wanted to experience God's strength in my weakness, but this remained an unfulfilled dream until I shared with others how I felt and allowed God to heal me from my wounds of the past. This was most clearly demonstrated for me when my coach and mentor, Mary Jones, who had encouraged me, prayed for my healing, prophesied over me, and apprenticed me into church leadership, died suddenly in Australia. I was encouraged to take a holiday in California for a month to grieve and come to terms with the tremendous sense of loss that I felt.

On my return from America I found that significant decisions had been made by the rest of the leadership team while I was away. One of those decisions was that all leading men including home group leaders would meet together, and this arrangement excluded me. I felt betrayed. Some of the men involved in this decision had been supported by me during times they had been going through a rough patch. Now, it seemed, I was not wanted in meetings where they claimed the men would share things that they could not share if a woman was present.

I tried to communicate my feelings, but the more I did so, the worse the situation became and the more my male colleagues became entrenched in their position. I continued to express my views, but each attempt left me feeling that they were unable, even unwilling to understand.

With hindsight I know that I was not being objective, and had over-reacted. I realise that my reaction had more to do with my past than the situation in which I found myself, and the Holy Spirit slowly uncovered the wounds of stinging injustice I had received long before this incident. There had been many occasions when I had felt excluded because I was not considered important enough to be told about a particular matter and once these were uncovered and healed, I was able to see the leadership issue objectively and to understand their perspective, and they mine. When their meetings had fulfilled their stated purpose, I was included once more.

We can either become embittered by life's painful experiences, or let God discipline us through them and shape our characters: 'The Lord disciplines those He loves . . . Endure hardship as discipline; God is treating you as sons . . . No discipline seems pleasant at the time, but painful. Later on, however, it produces a harvest of righteousness and peace for those who have been trained by it' (Hebrews 12. 7–11).

Early in my life I had decided that the best form of defence was attack. Someone once remarked: 'God has put a fighter in you.' I have needed this fighter-spirit in order to survive. From years of trauma, recounted in chapter one, life had been a continual battle to survive. I learned to fight back, at times with hostility or fear, and often feeling very much alone. I never really knew the real me because whenever I tried to express myself I was ridiculed.

In recent years I have been aware of God's refining

process and his desire to hone this fighter-spirit into perseverance and endurance. Only God knows how much progress I have made, but I can see that as a pioneer, I need to persist and be resilient. The difference now is that the hostility and fear I once had has largely been replaced by a more loving attitude and a sense of security.

Several years ago I found my job as church leader very difficult for a number of reasons. Leadership is never easy but the fact that I am a woman makes it more of an uphill task. Popular opinion in the new House Churches did not favour my position, and there were some hostile reactions not only from men but women too. I was constantly aware that I could be disqualified from leadership at any time either because my opinions were too strong, or because I was too emotional. I was the kind of person who, if someone did not understand me, would persist relentlessly until they understood, and I have retained some of that characteristic to this day, but in the majority of instances without so much of the heat!

When the church had guest preachers, I never knew what they might say about women leaders and in the first two years of my leadership I was excluded from invitations to leaders conferences, and left out of much that was happening. Both men and women were trying to come to terms with my leadership, and their reactions were not always helpful. There were frequent discussions between them and the male leaders, and I felt left on the outside, while they were on the inside talking about me. Others would talk to me directly, which I found much easier. But my two colleagues, Phil Vogel and Terry Brewer, defended me on many occasions. The constant questioning was draining and continued until my third year in leadership within Guildford Community Church.

There were hostile reactions from women in the

church, and I had to be careful if I was working with their husbands, or needed to meet with them for some reason. I had to ask the wives' permission to see their husbands, whereas if a male leader wanted to see the woman, he never needed to ask similar permission. I am glad to say that this situation no longer exists and over a period of years relationships of trust have been built up.

Two years after the start of Guildford Community Church it was not unusual for me to be counselling for up to fifty hours a week. I began to feel that it would be helpful to gather people together in small groups for ministry and it was agreed that I could do this with some of the women. The men felt that their wives needed help so they were more than happy for me to gather them together for this purpose. As a result many of the women were helped, healed and changed, and their husbands were envious when they saw the results. They began to ask if they could be a part of these groups. Of course, at the time, I was the only person able to lead these kind of groups and found myself leading men's gatherings as well.

The result of this time was that the men became aware that they had deep feelings too. They began to understand themselves much better, to the extent that their relationships and the way they treated others, not least their wives, was deeply challenged. They learned that the past has a direct bearing on present reactions, and they were led to forgive and receive forgiveness and healing and learn to express grief. This also changed the way they viewed me and my role as a leader. I was accepted for who I was and appreciated for the ministry God had given to me.

During this difficult time it was vital for me to share my personal battles with others, to receive God's healing, to be forgiven and to forgive. I believe it is important for everyone to share their struggles with trusted friends, because very often these struggles can stem from our own innate weaknesses which we are not able to see without help from other people. This frequently means revealing areas of our lives which we would rather keep hidden, believing them to be unacceptable. This is true vulnerability and means that the Holy Spirit has access to the root causes of our problems and is able to put His strength into our weaknesses. A likely consequence is that we shall be more aware of our own frailties and how much the grace of God has accomplished for us. In being conscious of our own weakness, we are more able to be tolerant towards what we see as other's imperfections, and therefore likely to be less prone to unforgiveness and roots of bitterness.

The changes were particularly noticeable in the lives of the men in Guildford Community Church. Their outlook on life and towards other people was changed. They became more aware of their feelings and saw that they were more emotional than they had realised. They conceded that many of their decisions apparently based on logic and objectivity, were in fact as 'emotional' as those of any woman!

Their attitude towards many of the women changed which helped them accept women into leadership. Realising that emotional disqualification was no disqualification as far as leadership was concerned, many of the men now discovered they were actually far more liable to react from hidden feelings than women.

Emotions, or lack of them, have nothing to do with our ability to cope with responsibility. Most of us do not find it easy to carry responsibility but if that is true for a man, it is more so for a woman. It seems to conflict with the trend of our society, our culture, our history, our psychology, and for many of us our past teaching. I believe that this has led many women to be reliant upon their husbands. Each one of us, however, is responsible for our own lives before God. All of us will face the Lord one day and be called to give an account of our individual response to Him. We shall not have husbands, wives, friends, or leaders to stand up and speak for us. We shall face our maker alone.

It is important for us all to know who we are and what God has called us to do. This seems especially true for women at this moment in history. Whereas encouragement from others is very important, sooner or later we must all be secure in the knowledge of our unique individuality that has its place in God's kingdom and that the tasks He has given us to do have been prepared by Him. God is faithful, and what He would like to see accomplished will happen, no matter how long it takes for mankind to respond:

'Many are the plans in a man's heart, but it is the Lord's purpose that prevails' (Proverbs 19.21).

4: Issues Need Not Divide Us

Another major concern of mine was that by exploring the role of women in leadership I was being potentially divisive. In recent years the people of God have desired unity, the need for which is so poignant that many men and women withdraw from controversial issues in the belief that the avoidance of disagreement aids unity. It is not conflict itself that divides us, but the absence of security and tolerance between people. Lack of tolerance is expressed when people are not secure enough in themselves to allow other people to be different. Not so long ago the issue of baptism in the Holy Spirit was considered divisive and it would seem that each new initiative by God is met with a wave of fear and prejudice.

The debate about women in leadership raises questions and strong feelings in the hearts and minds of many people. They feel a number of issues need to be discussed, considered and clarified, and the church is notorious for letting issues become real bones of contention. Despite this, no issue need divide the body of Christ.

There are men and women who have studied the Scriptures with integrity, searching thoroughly and with an open mind, who yet have genuine reservations concerning aspects of women in leadership. Despite those differences, however, those of us who believe women need to be given the opportunity to lead can still have fellowship with those who have reservations. The question is, will we? Our relationships would be very limited if restricted only to those with whom we were in total agreement. Married couples might find life a little difficult, and in the final analysis we might remain in fellowship with God alone, but who knows how long even that would last?

I have found it more difficult to respond objectively to people who appear prejudiced against women, because I feel that I am responding to a reaction on their part, rather than a genuine question. There seem to be no easy answers to this problem of prejudice, but I have found it useful to try and understand how the roots of prejudice grow in our lives.

We all have prejudices, but very seldom recognise them in ourselves. Only when we are faced with a situation which tests our views and innermost feelings are our prejudices exposed. I used to believe that I was not racist, but was challenged when I visited France for the first time. I found that I had a low opinion of French people for no particular reason, except that one of my past authority figures constantly referred to the French in a derogatory way. I could only think that subconsciously this had affected me and coloured my thoughts and feelings. My only recourse was to seek forgiveness and cleansing.

Our prejudices often extend to the male/female stereotype and these have roots as deep as any other. I would like to suggest four possible causes:

1. *Past relationships.* Stressful relationships make their mark on our lives and often leave a residue that can affect us for the rest of our days. An overbearing father, a dominant mother or a harsh teacher can cause us to have an unfavourable opinion of one or other sex. We can even become biased about certain names. We dislike a name simply because someone of that name mistreated us at some point in the past.

2. *Traumatic events*. Events such as sexual abuse, parental divorce or separation leave deep wounds within us. The publicity that has been given to child abuse in recent years, and subsequent interviews with victims on television, have shown only too graphically the very deep emotional trauma that is caused. Prejudice towards the men who, in the main, commit such acts is highlighted and this can extend to men in general. If wounds such as these remain unhealed, they can so easily develop into deep and lasting bitterness, which harms the individual concerned most of all. The resultant prejudice is perhaps understandable, but all the more unhealthy given its painful roots.

3. *Past conditioning*. We are all affected, consciously or subconsciously, by what we see and hear. Generally speaking our culture favours men, and this has a profound effect upon us all. Only recently I listened to a young man talking excitedly about the birth of his first child. He wanted a boy because he knew his own father would prefer a grandson.

Most of us assume that the bad driver in front of us is a woman. Many derogatory terms such as 'Cow', 'Bitch', 'Tart', 'Whore', 'Slut' are feminine. How often have we heard the comment 'You silly old woman' levelled at others, despite the fact they may be male? I am convinced that the more we come into contact with, and are exposed to prejudice towards people or groups, the more likely we are to pick up similar attitudes. Little wonder then, in our male orientated society that our children grow up with ingrained chauvinistic attitudes.

4. *Past teaching*. A long time ago I belonged to a church were we were taught that women should not hold positions of leadership. Despite my own inner conviction that this was not right, I went through a period when my own attitude itself became prejudiced against the leadership of women. Unaware of the fact,

I had imbibed an attitude from the leaders of the church that it was wrong for women to hold responsibility. I had even witnessed a deaconess being removed from her position because of the leadership stance on this matter. I had not consciously formulated my views in this realm, or researched the subject for myself, and because my loyalty was very strong, I would not have considered questioning the decision of the leaders.

One particular incident made me aware of my feelings. A friend, a man to whom I will be forever grateful, invited me to a meeting at which Jean Darnell was to preach. I was horrified that a woman should be speaking and at first refused to go. Eventually my friend persuaded me otherwise.

I arrived at the meeting feeling distinctly uncomfortable. As Jean Darnell spoke directly into people's lives through the operation of the gifts of the Spirit, it became very clear to me that the anointing of the Holy Spirit was upon her. It was obvious that authority from God was invested in the speaker and she was a woman! If the anointing of God was upon her, who was I to argue? Despite my theories and past teaching I was deeply challenged and came out of that meeting totally changed. My prejudice had been dealt with in one fell swoop. I realised that I had destroyed my own integrity, and allowed myself to be influenced by teaching with which, in my heart of hearts, I knew I did not agree. That one meeting redeemed that.

Some use the argument that God uses women when there is no man willing to be used. If men were available, he would use them, but as it is, he has to use second rate material. Women are only second best. I believe that such an argument is a slight on men, women and God himself. On men because it assumes that they do not wish to be used of God; on women because of the obvious emphasis on their being second choice; and on God because it dares to suggest that one of his chosen servants is being used only because He couldn't persuade the right person to do the job.

Our attitudes are often formulated subconsciously. There are many reasons for this, but two I have found to be most common are concerns about being acceptable to friends, and misplaced loyalty to leaders.

Peer pressure to conform can be enormous. A child can grow up in a multi-racial environment, for example, and think nothing of the fact that he or she is mixing with children of different races, cultures and colours, but let them fall into a group of kids that is exclusively one race, and very likely they will begin to hear derogatory remarks about children from other races. Within a very short time they will be under pressure to think as the majority, make similar remarks, and be seen to be 'one of the gang'. Their attitudes will change very quickly, simply in order to be acceptable.

This type of experience is mirrored time after time in all forms of prejudice, and is not just a childhood phenomenon. We adults know only too well, if we are honest with ourselves, just how difficult it is to resist peer pressure, the need to conform to the majority view in order to remain acceptable to, and accepted by, the group.

People who believe in faithfulness and loyalty often have tremendous struggles to believe that the view they hold is valid, especially if that view is different from the opinion of church leaders. There can be a misplaced sense of loyalty towards leaders when we feel that they must always be right because they are 'more spiritual' than us.

In the early days of the House Church movement, when the emphasis on authority and submission was strong, it was not unusual to hear the kind of teaching that implied that leaders were usually right. This left little room for individual thought, and diverging opinions were viewed in a negative light, verging on rebellion and unsubmissiveness. In some circles this attitude remains and only individuals with a great deal of courage can approach a strong leader with an alternative point of view.

We all want to be loved and accepted. Conflict causes problems because we are left wondering if people still love and accept us for who we are, or whether it is simply our conformity that makes us acceptable. These feelings can easily cause us to swallow our own opinion, and as a result imbibe attitudes and views with which we do not agree at first, though subsequently we may come to accept as our own.

I was once involved in a debate about a church's future. Members of the leadership put forward their views, and others were given the opportunity to express their feelings. I took the microphone at the meeting and questioned the ideas of two of the elders, suggesting that perhaps some reassessment might be necessary. I simply asked if there might not have been some mistake on a certain point. After the meeting, I overheard one of them say, 'We can see what Bren is made of, because she has no fear of standing and challenging the Lord's anointed.'

There is a spiritual dimension to such prejudice. Our arch enemy, the devil, has been particularly opposed to women since the garden of Eden. Enmity between men and women was a result of the fall: 'And I will put enmity between you and the woman, and between your offspring and hers; he will crush your head, and you will strike his heel'(Genesis 3.15). Significantly not only did a woman's seed eventually defeat Satan, but the seed of any woman who seeks to be obedient to the Lord is also potentially victorious over our enemy. With the authority invested in us by Jesus, we can be released from the bondage of our history, and into the freedom for which Christ bought us – including unity between the sexes.

These forces, pressures and circumstances, among others, can create within us a negative opinion of some types of people and their views before the true situation is understood. We become intolerant of another's approach to life, their interpretations of Scripture and consequent lifestyle.

Initially my position as a woman in authority provoked some interesting reaction, including aggression, much of which stemmed from fear. At the time there was much stress placed upon unity among the saints, the need for us all to be of one heart and one mind, living in harmony and showing our oneness to the world. When some people said that they would leave the church if we continued to advocate women in leadership, I had to resolve the question as to whether or not I was being divisive. It was no light matter to be the possible cause of division in the body of Christ, and this caused me a lot of heartache and soulsearching. I found it very hard not to react out of frustration, disappointment and guilt. Many times the thought plagued me, 'If I were not in leadership, perhaps they would never have left.'

I had to work very hard to win people. When I began to teach in a group, I was aware that some would not be prepared to listen because I was a woman. I tried to be gracious and win people from a place of integrity, not through manipulation of any kind. I knew in my heart that issues need not divide us, that conflict does not necessarily have to mean separation. The cause of such problems is our inability to stay with each other even if we hold different interpretations of Scripture. We only face an impasse when we are intolerant of one another's views, and are unable to see that people can differ with integrity.

Some prejudice, even if not acceptable, is understandable. There are often legitimate reasons for animosity towards another, stemming from deep wounds. For a good deal of the time, however, our prejudices and fears are irrational, and cannot be eradicated by argument or even good theology. They will only be dealt with effectively when we openly recognise our own partialities, and willingly allow the grace of the Holy Spirit to work in us.

Fear is often at the root of our prejudices. When challenged with different views, we can become insecure and fearful because our safe and well-tried boundaries appear to be threatened. In this respect I think that men are afraid of losing their masculinity. Generally speaking they have been conditioned to believe that they are the dominant sex, and therefore need to be in that position if they are not to feel threatened.

It is interesting to observe a large group of men and women together. Both men and women will talk to men more readily than women, actually recognising that maleness is superior. It is not necessarily conscious, but I have noticed on more than one occasion that this is the case at leader's gatherings. Maleness is viewed more highly than femaleness, and this becomes quickly apparent if they are three leaders in a room, one of whom is female. The woman will usually find that she is spoken to least often by the others present.

This was why Jesus was so revolutionary, because He spent time with women. He gave his full attention to the woman at the well of Sychar and saw this as equally important as talking to Nicodemus or any of the disciples. The position of women had reached an all time low in Jesus' day and He shows clearly that He is the destroyer of prejudicial barriers by not only talking to a woman, but a Samaritan woman (and one of questionable character at that!) with whom the Jews would never mix.

There can be little doubt after even a superficial glance at church history that there are many different interpretations of Scripture. Only security in God will produce the tolerance we need to bear with one another's differences.

The role of women need not produce schism, but our lack of forbearance with one another will. If at the end of the day it is not possible for someone to resolve the position of women in leadership, it would be better for them to find a place in which they can be comfortable. If the problem becomes one of conscience, and the person feels that the issue is warring against all they believe God is saying to them, then I would reluctantly have to agree that they should find somewhere else to worship and serve God.

Forcing the pace

Prejudice is not alone in causing division. Reaction plays its fair share. There are many women who are utterly frustrated by what they see as the lack of progress in equal opportunities everywhere and as a result try to force the pace. Equally there are men who are fearful of the implications of this and consequently try to prevent the development of a woman.

Both are reactions that can cause a lot of harm. Radical feminism, the movement that was initiated in the early sixties is perhaps an example of this. Their objectives include the abolition of the nuclear family and the right to be open about sexual preferences. There is much talk about 'sisterhood', the 'myth' of real love and the promotion of artificial reproduction in order to free women from reliance upon men they resent. These ideals seem to reflect strong anti-male attitudes. It is likely that this style of feminism has engendered mistrust, making many of us reticent to consider the role of women in society and the church, lest we become reactionary ourselves, fall into similar traps, and become numbered among them.

The word feminist produces shudders in many people. It has almost become a term of abuse. I have heard female church leaders called feminists, but I suspect that people do not really understand the meaning of the term. If challenged, they would probably not mean radical feminism. It is important for us to understand that there are different shades of feminism. If we are going to use the term, we need to be clear about its meaning.

I know a woman leader who regularly speaks at large conferences, who has been labelled 'the feminist'. She is no more a feminist than I am, but simply a female leader who has strong views. She is not advocating radical feminism! In my view many feminists are extreme. They promote womens' superiority and are often described as men haters. There is no point in displacing men simply by believing in 'woman power'. My heart cry is for equality, not domination by either of the sexes.

Women still face an enormous mountain to climb, and God alone can help them to find the way. Having said that, I do believe that for too long the church has followed the world in its established patterns of male elitism. Although it is unlikely that every church will rush to accept a policy of women in leadership, it is important that we are at least aware of the tensions which may arise when women are not allowed to function in the same way as men.

One of the most perplexing areas for a career woman is the apparent dichotomy between what she does in the world of business, and what she is allowed to do in the church. Of course, it does not necessarily follow that someone in a responsible position in business should automatically hold such a position in the church, either male or female. But there are women whose leadership qualities have been recognised at their workplace who have been given authority over men and who are clearly anointed to lead in church as well.

I knew such a woman who in her work as a city banker was head of a department which included men. In her local church, however, she was taught that women should not have authority over men. This caused a tremendous conflict and tension within her and she felt that her opinions were not valued by the male leaders of her church. She had expected to receive understanding and a willing ear from them, but found she received more support and encouragement from her bosses and colleagues at work. After many years of struggling to be understood and gain some acceptance she gave up and became disillusioned, leaving that particular church. Only God knows whether her feelings were valid or not, but certainly frustration occurs in many women who find there is little or no opportunity for ministry or leadership within their local fellowship, when the world seems to recognise their abilities and make room for them.

Women in leadership sometimes find that their position is used as a convenient hook on which to hang disillusionment or frustration, for example, 'We are not growing as a church because we have got a woman in leadership here', or, 'God is not blessing us because we are allowing a woman to minister'. All too often this is used as an excuse to leave the church. I would like to re-emphasise, however, that female leadership need not cause separation, if there is sufficient tolerance for varying interpretations of Scripture and different expressions of church.

Those who promote women in leadership are often accused of causing division within the church. The truth is that those who encourage men and women to work together in *all* areas of church life are those who are more likely to bring about unity and reconciliation between the sexes.

5: Breaking The Mould

Fundamentally, the New Testament teaches that authority can only be given, not taken. Women and men therefore both need each other in order to develop their gifts and fulfil their potential and calling before God. Certainly this was true for me and because the majority of church leaders are still male, most women will need other men to allow them to assume a leadership role. In my own experience the support and encouragement of a number of men has helped establish me in a leadership position. In addition to help from men, however, there is also a great need among women for female role-models.

The role of women in the Church has provoked a great deal of debate. It features significantly in almost every denomination and the controversy has even aroused the interest of the media. Hardly a week goes by without an article appearing in the national press, and it is rapidly becoming a highly contentious issue.

Few people would contest that Church government, the business world, and much of society is male dominated. I do not believe that this is God's ideal, or adequately reflects life as it should be in His kingdom. Our thinking is still dominated by the traditional roles of men and women. Men are considered to be breadwinners, the leaders, the hunters, the go-getters and the masters, and responsible for their wives and families. Whereas I believe that to be partly true, I also believe that primarily we are answerable to God for our own lives. Each person must one day give account to God as individuals, not as someone else's wife, son, daughter, or even husband.

At one point in our own church's development we felt it was important to establish the principal of individual responsibility. Whenever we wanted to communicate with church members we sent separate letters to couples so that wives began to feel valued as individuals and not just as appendages to their husbands. How many times, I wonder, has a woman been introduced to people, either at a social occasion, or a Christian meeting, as 'so-and-so's wife'?

There are still very few women in positions where they are able to influence the direction of the Church to any great degree. This applies equally to some of the newer churches who claim to be on the cutting edge of what God is wanting to do in our nation. While there has been debate, conferences and seminars on the subject, very few groups have either wanted, or been able, to open up the way for women to fulfil their God-given roles.

If this is to be challenged and changed we must find ways of establishing new patterns. I believe there are a number of important keys that could unlock the status quo if given serious consideration not only by those of us in the new fellowships, but also by Christians of other traditions.

1. Encouragement and opportunity

Since male precedence is so firmly established, women need courage to challenge the accepted norm. Ideally both women and men are equipped to give and receive authority. Since at present leadership is predominantly male, the ball is firmly in their court to acknowledge this and to release women into the ministries to which

God has called them. As frustrated as many women are by continual struggles facing them, it is unusual to find a woman forcing her way into a role, even if she is convinced that God has anointed and gifted her for the task.

There are some male leaders who acknowledge and support women in leadership but tacit agreement alone is not enough to launch them into leadership. These men must provide the platform from which women operate. At present this is a very rare occurrence!

Over the last fifteen years, the Holy Spirit has focussed attention on aspects of church life that have been neglected: relationships; plurality of leadership; worship; service and commitment, to name but a few. The issue of women in leadership is poised to figure prominently in the next decade and must be faced.

When Terry Brewer began to lead our church team, he gave me the opportunity to lead publicly. I began to speak and teach in meetings, direct worship and fulfil the roles that you would expect of a church leader. The support of my male colleagues in the leadership team was crucial to me. They were strategic in 'paving the way' for others to accept my role, and were particularly careful to see that I was at ease in predominantly male gatherings. Terry would also, on different occasions, publicly confirm that he believed that what I was saying was from God and should be listened to. We were aware that this was breaking new ground, and could be misinterpreted, criticised or even opposed. We also acknowledged, however, that this was inevitable.

2. Personal responsibility and calling

One of the hallmarks for which we at Guildford Community Church have become known is the way we have tried to encourage a sense of personal responsibility. Every human being is precious to God in their own right, their sex and marital status are secondary. A growing trend towards humanism in our society has not encouraged personal accountability. We are victims of circumstance and our environment, shaped by all our experiences from birth, and therefore not ultimately responsible for the decisions that we make, or the actions that we take. Very often the reason for an action has become the excuse for it. Whereas there are good reasons for certain kinds of behaviour, these should not become excuses for our negative reactions.

This philosophy of life conflicts with the overriding tenor of Scripture, which teaches us to answer for our responses and reactions. Indeed there can be no reconciliation and relationship with God until we are willing to accept this principle. In the final analysis God has given us life and with it free will to exercise as we choose. No one else can live our lives for us, no matter how close they are or what position they hold.

This principle has affected the methods we have used when conducting our church affairs. For example, we have not made the assumption that because a leader is married, their partner automatically has that same calling or ability. In the past, when leadership was exclusively male, this was not a problem. Once women become part of the equation the tables are turned, and the issues become more highly charged. Men whose wives are leaders can feel threatened and insecure. Somehow their masculinity is undermined, and there is a tendancy to worry about their image. One only needs to observe the way husbands of women in the public eye are caricatured by the media to understand how this arises.

We have tried to be sensitive to partners of leaders whether they are men or women whilst, at the same time stressing that *both* are not necessarily called to be leaders. Only those with the appointment to lead should carry responsibility. Husbands of wives who are leading would not be expected to shoulder responsibility, neither, therefore, should wives of husbands in leadership.

Where the potential for conflict has existed in the home when either the husband or wife has been left behind, we have found that tensions can be eased and problems surmounted by ensuring frequent communication. It is very important that the partner who is not a leader knows how valuable they are to us and the church as a whole, so that we can foster strong relationships between everyone concerned. In this way any problems arising are far more likely to be overcome.

3. The willingness to assume responsibility

Women must be prepared to shoulder responsibility when it is offered to them. It is not always an easy thing to do. From my discussions with women I have counselled, it has become apparent that many do not believe they have the necessary aptitude for leadership or even the confidence to handle situations on their own. Clearly there are several reasons for their reluctance, the most obvious being past teaching. Many were taught as young Christians that the function of a leader was not appropriate for women. As a result of this, hopes and aspirations were repressed as they sought to be obedient to what they believed God was saying. The last thing they wanted was to be accused of rebellion and disobedience to the teaching of Scripture.

Now, new light is being thrown on the subject, and, as the Church is being challenged to think through the matter, women are facing opposition because of past teaching. Many have submerged their own gifting and calling in an attempt to submit themselves to men, only to find that Scripture does not demand this in respect to all men, simply to their husbands if they are married. As they consider the new found possibilities, many are insecure and unsure. There is no doubt that women are equipped to carry authority. This is ably demonstrated in some parts of the church today, throughout history, in contemporary society, and perhaps most importantly in the Scriptures.

Miriam, for example, led Israel with Moses and Aaron: '. . . I sent Moses to lead you, also Aaron and Miriam' (Micah 6.4b). God clearly demonstrates that he holds both Aaron and Miriam responsible and accountable to Him judging them both for the misdemeanour that was committed:

'Then the Lord came down in a pillar of cloud . . . and summoned Aaron and Miriam . . . The anger of the Lord burned against them, and he left them. When the cloud lifted from above the Tent, there stood Miriam – leprous, like snow. Aaron turned towards her and saw that she had leprosy; and he said to Moses, "Please my lord, do not hold against us the sin that we have so foolishly committed . . .". So Moses cried out to the Lord, "Oh God, please heal her!"' (Numbers 12. 5–13).

It is obvious from this incident that God not only deems women to be responsive, but responsible and answerable to Him for their actions. I have found this understanding of God's perspective helpful.

It is important, not only for women to be secure in God's calling if they are to combat this hesitancy for leadership, but also for them to receive reinforcement and recognition from leaders and friends of their calling. Someone once suggested that I could test my call by considering five points:

a) *The witness of my own heart.* As we are united with Christ by His Spirit, so His desires become ours. As I looked at my own feelings about leadership, was there an overriding sense of peace in my heart about what I perceived as God's call on my life?

b) *The witness of my peers.* It is rarely a good thing to make decisions in isolation. As I shared my thoughts for the future with my close and trusted friends, what was their reaction and response?

c) *The witness of the word of God.* Whatever I believed the future was going to hold I needed to have a clear confirmation from Scripture.

d) *The witness of my church leaders.* Naturally I respected people called by God who were already leading, and wanted their opinion about my calling. Scripture clearly teaches that we are to submit to our leaders' authority, whether or not they agree with us, provided we are not asked to do something that is clearly against our conscience, or against Scripture or immoral.

e) *The witness of my personal circumstances.* Although we cannot allow circumstances to dictate our lives, God can use them to guide us, or at the very least give us clues as to His intentions. I had to ask whether God's hand was discernible in my circumstances, and whether they were clearly leading me down a particular path.

It is vital we check our calling in this way and allow others to test it from the very beginning. Unless we are certain of God's purposes for our lives, there is little possibility we will withstand the pressures that will surely come.

There have been times when I have wanted to give up, withdraw in anger, react and resort to retaliation. The belief in God's call and the knowledge that my calling was tested and confirmed from the very start have given me strength to carry on.

Although encouragement from others is important, sooner or later we must build on our own foundation of the knowledge that we are important to God's kingdom, and that the tasks He has given us to do have been prepared especially for us by His hand.

4. Our use of language

Words we use and how we use them can have a powerful reinforcing effect and even if we are not always aware of the process, they can actually add fuel to the fire of our prejudices. Language is potent and leaves impressions for good or evil in people's minds.

Studies of language have been carried out in the workplace with a view to eliminating the reinforcement of stereotyping. An advertisement may read for example: 'We require a receptionist for our busy sales office. She must be able to type well, have a good telephone manner etc.' From this one sentence it is clear there is an assumption that the receptionist will be female. This is a small example to illustrate how preconceived ideas are held by people of both sexes.

In some cases, perhaps, the process has gone too far, for example in the building industry, which is notoriously chauvinistic, there were a few ripples caused when suggestions were made that the word 'manhole' should be replaced by 'access chamber'. There is no doubting those who wanted to take the whole exercise to an unacceptable extreme, but nevertheless the use of language needs to be given careful consideration, not least in the Church.

Although I believe that the whole of Scripture is the word of God, there are many examples of sexist translations of the text. Seemingly insignificant details can have far reaching consequences. The word 'brothers' is often used in the Bible where the term 'believers' would actually be more accurate. In his letter to the Thessalonians, Paul writes about knowing our calling: 'Believers loved by God, we know that he has chosen you . . .' (1 Thessalonians 1.4).

There are many other similar examples in the New Testament (Revelation 19.10; Romans 1.13; Acts 1.15;

Acts 6.3; Matthew 28.10; Hebrews 2.17 and Romans 9.3). Nowhere is this more noticeable than in the letter to the Hebrews. The NIV translates Hebrews 13.17 as 'Obey your leaders and submit to their authority. They keep watch over you as men who must give account'. The original Greek word here translated as men does in fact leave the gender open. The word could easily refer to either men or women. Similarly the chapter continues, in verse 22, with 'Brothers I urge you to bear with my word of exhortation . . .'. The word translated as 'brothers', should in fact be 'brethren', a term that has come to refer increasingly to men, but originally was an all-inclusive term for men and women.

I have sat in many meetings where it is apparent from language used that leadership is generally assumed to be male . . . 'When a leader comes home to his wife . . .' and 'We need strong men to lead the church . . .' or 'We would like you to pray about this weekend conference for leaders and their wives . . .'. It is unlikely that the people concerned are aware of their words or the effect they are having. This reveals underlying attitudes, however, and only reinforces the status quo – what has been will always be. Women as a result can feel shunned, disregarded, excluded and inferior.

Very few of us are innocent in our use of language to reinforce stereotypes, because we have grown up in an environment that constantly confirms them. Our attitudes are important. We need to realise what we are doing and make a special effort not to use sexist language. This is just as important for men because women can also be equally guilty of sexual bias. We can all fall into the same traps. Recently at one meeting a colleague remarked, 'Listen to all those men cackling like a bunch of old women!'.

Generally speaking, though, a new sensitivity is emerging amongst men which is beginning to have an effect and to challenge others. In society there seems to be a growing awareness, not only in the area of language, but in the realm of image and stereotypes. Media images are changing with women beginning to be represented outside the domestic setting. We now have advertisements to reflect the changing role of women in the business world, for example, and programmes which show women accepted into employment previously reserved for men such as engineering and mechanics.

In my own church and perhaps elsewhere I have been encouraged by the fact that my male colleagues will no longer accept invitations to male only conferences. We feel this has helped to break new ground in the realm of acceptable practice.

5. The acceptance of singleness

If it has been a challenge to be a woman leader it has been even more so because I am unmarried. This created further barriers in as far as the commonly held concept of a leader was concerned. I suspect that this was, and still perhaps is, connected with a prevailing attitude towards singleness. I remember a church member whose husband happened to be a leader, and who, in my opinion should have known better saying, 'We don't have many single women in our church, all the good ones have been taken.'

I believe that we need to reassess our understanding of singleness. We live in a society which is marriage orientated despite the fact that it is not viewed as the binding covenant it once was. Marriage is seen as a status symbol and regarded as a sign of maturity. To have been married and now be divorced is almost more acceptable than never having been married at all.

This attitude is no less prevalent in the church. I am certainly not criticizing the emphasis that is given to maintaining healthy marriages and family life, but this has almost developed to the extent that an unmarried person is a slightly inferior being. A couple of centuries ago, there was an emphasis in the church in favour of people remaining single, but that was also taken to an extreme, and balance had to be restored. Today, I believe, there is an equal need for a balance to be redressed.

The Bible refers to the single state as an equally honourable way to live as the married state (1 Corinthians 7). The silent message in our culture seems to be, 'If you are unmarried you must either be odd, a misfit or perhaps even homosexual, but at the very least my suspicion is aroused'. To some extent this has filtered through into the church affecting our view of singleness, and our attitude to people who are unmarried. If we meet an older person who is single, probably many of us ask the question, albeit silently, 'Why are they still alone?'

Singleness is seen by many as not only second class and less than God's ideal, but also a lifestyle that lacks experience and, therefore, disqualifies from leadership and ministry. Brochures that arrive on my desk advertising seminars for leaders and their wives not only exclude female leaders, but also the unmarried, whether male or female.

In the Jewish patriarchal society, marriage was the only reasonable state for an adult to contemplate, but in the New Testament Jesus ushers in a new order. He says to his disciples: '. . . Not everyone can accept this teaching, but only those to whom it has been given. For some are eunuchs because they were born that way; others were made that way by men; and others have renounced marriage because of the kingdom of heaven. The one who can accept this should accept it' (Matthew 19. 11–12).

Both celibacy and monogamy are promoted by Jesus and reflect the coming age when the Messiah will establish his kingdom. Marriage reflects the great wedding supper to come of Jesus and his bride, the Church; celibacy mirrors the fact that there will be no marriage in Jesus' new kingdom. Paul expresses his personal view to the Christians at Corinth when he writes: 'So then he who marries the virgin does right, and he who does not marry her does even better' (1 Corinthians 7.38).

In the kingdom of God there is no competition between marriage and singleness. One is not more important than nor superior to the other. They are both honourable and God-ordained. I feel certain, however, that God wants to lift singleness out of the pit into which it has fallen, not in order to downgrade marriage, but to upgrade the single lifestyle. I venture to say the church, apart perhaps from the Catholic church, has made singleness a difficult path to follow. Miriam, Elijah, Elisha, Daniel, probably Paul and certainly John the Baptist, Mary and her sister Martha, Lazarus and Jesus himself, as far as we know, were all single.

I have found that to embrace singleness as a gift from God has released His grace into my life. By that I mean that accepting my single state has been the key to finding peace within myself. God knows my needs, and He meets them. I accept that He knows what is best for me, and as a result I am able to see the positive side of being single and use it to serve God. I have definite advantages over married people in terms of freedom even if it means that at a personal level I may lose out in some areas. I have not committed myself to a lifetime of singleness; I only know that this is my present state, and I want to use the time to full advantage. I often say, 'Today some are married, who knows for how long? Today some are single, who knows for how long?'

Singleness and the role of the single person in the life of the church needs to be understood. It is neither a qualification nor a disqualification for leadership. Being unmarried has both advantages and limitations, but has nothing to do with someone's maturity or ability to lead.

6. Challenging tradition

Some aspects of church life are more firmly steeped in tradition than others. Much of it is helpful, while some can have a negative effect and prove a barrier to what God wants to achieve. There is nothing wrong with tradition provided it has not lost its life and meaning. For example, many of the customs surrounding a wedding ceremony have lost their meaning for the majority of people. Some claim to be able to trace much of the tradition including bridesmaids, ushers, best man, confetti and wedding cake, back to biblical roots, but most of this is lost in the 20th century. That, notwithstanding, I venture to ask how many of us would expect a woman to officiate?

I remember wondering how the couple would respond when my team leader asked me to officiate at their wedding. They were a little unsure about the prospect at first, but once we started meeting together to prepare, all uncertainty was dispelled. After the ceremony the ridiculous thought ran through my mind, 'Did the couple feel married?'. I was relieved when they told me they did and still do!

Having officiated at many weddings since then, I can look back and smile at my reticence, for it is God who binds a man and woman together. Nevertheless it seemed to me that conducting a wedding was clearly breaking with tradition and was a significant milestone in my own life, and the life of our church.

Aspects of church traditions can be unhelpful, but because they have become so deeply entrenched in our thinking it has become almost unthinkable to change them. Those that obstruct the onward move of God's Spirit are sacred cows that need to be placed firmly on the altar of sacrifice. At the very least there must be a willingness to persevere and persist until there is change.

7. Practical application

A good friend of mine often used the catch phrase: 'Doing it is doing it.' We can get so caught up with pet theories and ideas of what ought to be, that we never actually get down to the nitty gritty tasks of implementing ideas and beliefs. There is a danger that we can agree with the principle of women in leadership, but never put it into practice.

It is not uncommon for women who are called by God to minister within the church, to find themselves prevented from doing so. I have lost count of the number of women who have recounted their stories with much pain, and there is overwhelming evidence that many are restricted from serving God in the way that He intended. Even if they are accepted onto leadership teams, it is often a struggle for them to become equals with men.

A woman told me that she was asked to sit on a committee composed entirely of men. She was there because of her ability, knowledge and expertise. When refreshments were brought into the meeting, the men would look at her, then at the food and drinks, then back to her, with the obvious expectation that it was the lady's place to serve them. Their automatic assumptions indicated a conditioning in their minds that she was not quite on a par with them.

Some women manage to find acceptable ways of ministering; acceptable that is, to the men they are working with, but this does not always alleviate their problem. Others find avenues for service elsewhere without the support of their local church and as a result become isolated and lonely. There is little doubt in my mind that the safest place for anyone to serve is with the assistance, backing and support of the local church, where we are known by a group of people who care for us with all our weaknesses and foibles. It is from the Christian community that we receive prayer, encouragement and support of a concrete nature, and we will need this more than ever if our circumstances demand perseverance and commitment of time and energy.

8. The price of pioneering

There is a high price to be paid by those who pioneer into new areas. Inevitable struggles that ensue can produce the very best in us, and bring out traits we were hardly aware of. They are often the agent for refining character, strengthening resolve to endure hardship and a determination to persevere whatever the odds. They also demand a great deal in terms of spiritual, emotional, mental and physical resources.

It is tragic when women who have struggled and fought against prevailing opinion for a long time in order to be able to express their natural and spiritual gifts in a church become so discouraged and disillusioned at the lack of acceptance and progress, that they resign themselves to second best, or even opt out of ministry altogether. I know women who believe that they have lost the battle for their ministry to be accepted, and feel that nothing will ever change. They have come to the point where they feel that opinion is simply too loaded against them. The barriers have been built so high that they can never overcome them, and they retreat to where they are no longer 'rocking the boat'.

Whatever the rights and wrongs of such a decision, it is understandable that women do withdraw under these circumstances. A natural human response to pain is to withdraw from the perceived source. Breaking new ground is hard work. There are discouragements, setbacks and disappointments and we all need respite from time to time, in order to be healed by the Lord where this is necessary, to receive strength from Him for a fresh initiative, and to have our faith and hope restored. Our vision can so easily be dimmed when for every step forward we make, at times we seem to take three backwards. We need time for vision to be renewed and there is, therefore, nothing wrong in retreating from the action now and again.

I hope with all of my heart that the majority of women who believe that God has called them to ministry and leadership will find the courage, faith and strength to continue with their efforts to see that calling accomplished. One of the greatest tragedies that could occur would be if women, after struggling to become a leader, then discourage or make it difficult for other women to join their ranks. I suspect that this is possible. The few women who have influence have a tremendous responsibility to ensure that others are encouraged and established in their God-appointed place.

Once a woman has struggled and fought for acceptance of her ministry, she may well want to be the 'kingpin' and remain so. In such a position it is easy to find ways to discourage and use her influence to prevent others from joining her. It only takes a few well-chosen words such as 'The women are not ready for such responsibility yet', or 'There simply aren't the women around ready to take on such a task' and this could be accepted by the majority of men because, to be truthful, it is probably what they want to hear.

Indisputably there are women ready and waiting, who are capable of leading and ministering, but who are not given the opportunity to do so. If their way is further blocked by a woman who has 'made it', there will be yet another mountain to climb and barrier to push down. I have seen this happening, and it is not a pretty sight; in fact it is a tragedy and will be a disaster as far as the hopes of many women are concerned.

Some women have found acceptable ways to minister, but where are the role models in terms of teachers, preachers, leaders of meetings, pastors, evangelists and apostles? Rather than promoting one another as women, we could so easily discredit each other, and that would be nothing short of a disaster. I pray we will find God's grace to encourage one another into whatever form of service he has prepared for us, regardless of sex.

There are encouraging signs in the British Church. A number of leading men have planted their feet firmly on the side of women in leadership and have produced equally convincing arguments from Scripture in their favour. These men have taken some risks in taking this stance and I am personally indebted to them.

There are a number of women leading smaller groups of various kinds within churches. Some share in the oversight of fellowships and a few have the responsibility of leading a church. The current openness to change has presented women with new possibilities to explore areas of responsibility which have previously been denied them. I believe that we could be approaching the days of women's greatest opportunity to express their God-given talents. All that is needed is a willingness to continue pioneering.

In conclusion

Women need to take up the challenge to serve in all aspects of church life, including those of teaching, preaching and leading. Nobody underestimates the difficulties that will be encountered in seeking to fulfil these rôles. I recall a prayer meeting where we were all encouraged to lead in prayer, but the volume of noise made by the men was so great that there would have been little possibility of most women being heard! Often these situations are unintentional. With increased awareness of the differences, and by co-operation, the problem of styles can be overcome. I have found that the majority of men, once they have been alerted to the problems, are very helpful and sensitive in these areas.

The lack of female role models means that it is difficult not to imitate currently accepted styles and patterns of leadership, which within the church are almost exclusively male. I do not want my style to be a carbon copy of someone elses. It is important that we all bring our unique personality and style of leadership to bear upon a given situation, without feeling that because it is different, it is inferior. I agree whole-heartedly with someone who once said, 'I am happy to work in a man's world, as long as I can be a woman in it'.

6: Our History. . . .

During my own journey through life, there have been times when a personal battle seemed to rage between me and the world. It became imperative to see this issue in context. The destructive confrontation between men and women is timeless. The tension between the sexes is a deep-seated and complex thread running throughout the history of humanity.

There have been occasions when I have felt very alone and tempted to give up. I have heard men talk about wanting women in leadership, but have actually seen little headway, and breakthroughs seem a long time in coming. There have been occasions when other leading women have challenged my leadership, or seemed threatened by it in some way. In certain contexts I have struggled, experienced some failure, and been opposed by people I thought were supporting me. I have initiated a number of principles of ministry and found God using them, but they have also been severely criticized and undermined at times by both men and women. At other times I have been discouraged. In all of these experiences, however, God has never failed to inspire and strengthen me.

I have often taken long walks into the hills alone and talked to God about my feelings and battles. On one such occasion I felt the Lord encourage me with words that remain etched on my memory: 'Look behind you and see those who are following.' Immediately I had a mental picture of many others treading the same path behind me. Until that moment I had not understood that I was helping to create a road on which others would be able to walk in the future.

This personal revelation has also been strengthened by the reassurance that I am not alone in the struggle. By studying records of women in the past, I realised that they too have been oppressed to some degree or other, and from as long ago as the garden of Eden have struggled to find their rightful place in society.

People today on the whole seem to live for the present. There is little thought given to what has been, or what might be in the future. Identity and purpose in life, however, is inextricably linked to our history, and to our destiny. I believe it is very important for women to have not only an appreciation of the past, but also the future as God sees it.

Western concepts of women have largely originated from Greek thought and ideas, where women were portrayed as romantic, beautiful, graceful and charming. Woe betide you if you were not any of these! The Greeks were monogamous and a woman's marriage was arranged by her father. Although she had no legal rights a married woman was held in high regard, despite the fact that her duties were mainly domestic, ordering the household, caring for and bringing up the children etc.

With the rise of Rome, women attained more social freedom because there was an abundance of Greek slaves to hand. Women who had reasonable intelligence and were wealthy, were educated. Generally speaking, however, they abused their freedom.

In Jesus' day, as we have already seen, the place of women had reached an all time low and they were synonymous in the Talmud books with slaves and minors. One observer states 'woman is a pitcher full of filth with its mouth full of blood.'

That women were inferior is clearly underlined by literature of all ages. The assumption was made that the expression of sexuality was all consuming and central to a woman's interest, and that they had little time or inclination left for anything else.

In the early centuries after Christ there was a widely held view that women had no soul. I thought this belief had disappeared around the sixth century when in Maçon, France, the council of churches had a debate on the subject and an ensuing vote on the motion 'Women have a soul' was carried by one vote. As late as the eighteenth century however some still believed women were 'soul-less'. Samuel Butler expressed it this way: 'The souls of women are so small that some believe they have none at all!'.

In the Middle Ages the church insisted that the soul of a woman was equal to that of a man, but because Eve was seen to be the instigator of the Fall, it was considered necessary for a woman to be under a man's authority.

Interpretation of the Scriptures by the early church fathers regarding women was fundamental in its shaping of Christian thinking in the Middle Ages. Because blame was laid upon Eve, all women were considered morally inferior to men. The Church's attitudes and actions were moulded accordingly. It was determined to stamp out witchcraft, and the existence of witches was generally believed to be proof of the carnal weakness of the female sex as a whole. Men were encouraged to fear and guard against this. It is my firm belief that fear lies at the root of much of our hostility and has lead to a deep distrust of both sexes by each other.

In those days, a man's priority was to marry, since a wife brought him land, helped him work his farm, ran the home and provided him with an heir. Daughters who married, might have to take land with them, but they could also be the means of building a closer alliance with the other family. In this way a woman's status would be shaped by her ability to bear children, a factor which contributed to the inseparable bond between marriage and property, the symbols of wealth and power.

The interests of past and future generations weighed heavily on a woman. It was a burden that proved greater in aristocratic circles, where land and family prestige were at stake. But even peasant families were proud and did all they could to protect or enrich their humble existence. A woman's freedom to choose whether or not to marry, when to marry and whom to marry were sacrificed to the benefit of family considerations at all levels. Women's roles were solely defined in terms of wife and mother, virgin or whore, nun or witch.

I can understand, having read a number of feminist writings, the reason for much of their anger. Holy Scripture was, they say, a means of justifying women's subordination and explaining her inferiority. Even as a copy of her Maker she was not a good one. She was not one of his best efforts!

Only in the nineteenth century did women begin to work together to fight for their emancipation. Perhaps the breakthrough came when girls were included in secondary education during the 1840s. Women were able to enter university from 1875 onwards, although it was not until 1948 that the bastion, Cambridge, conceded to graduate women on an equal basis with men.

The advent of the Industrial Revolution brought some affluence to the middle classes and some unmarried women began to agitate for admission to the professions, which would alone guarantee them an income and a standing which corresponded with their social status. In order to do that, they needed the necessary political power to force legislative changes which would entitle them to enter university. Thus began the campaign for voting rights.

The rise of pressure groups, beginning with the suffrage societies, largely instigated the above changes. Feminism was the name given to one of these movements. It was defined as 'The doctrine of equal rights for women based on the theory of the equality of the sexes'. The name came into English usage in this sense in the 1890s, replacing the term womanism, meaning the qualities of women.

Feminism has received a bad press and some are tempted to dismiss its extreme views completely. Before these are discarded entirely, however, it is important for us to understand that the rise of such groups eventually brought about hard-won changes. Though today we may suspect radical feminism, the feminists of the late 1800s are to be thanked for the achievement of positive changes, which have brought a more balanced status to women in the law of this land. The Divorce Act of 1857, for example, whilst allowing a husband to divorce his wife on grounds of adultery, required her to prove him guilty of rape, sodomy or bestiality, or of adultery in conjunction with incest, bigamy, cruelty or desertion. Only continual pressure has brought about the necessary changes.

Although suffrage societies had been formed since the mid 1800s, it was not until 1903 that Mrs. Pankhurst and two of her daughters, Christabel and Sylvia, founded the WSPP (Women's Social and Political Party). Its main objective was to be independent of any political party and persuade electors to vote against any Parliamentary candidate who refused to consider votes for women.

To coincide with the opening of Parliament in 1908, the Suffragettes held a three day women's Parliament.

On the third day, the 13th February, Mrs. Pankhurst, armed with a rolled resolution and a few lily of the valley flowers, led a deputation to the Prime Minister. Soon after starting out, she was arrested. She was the first of many and there were numerous demonstrations, not without violence, destruction and arson. Women prisoners were not treated well, and in fact, at one point were ordered to be force fed after an attack on a procession that included the Prime Minister.

The General Election of 1910 brought an opportune halt to militancy. All Suffragette efforts were concentrated on campaigning against the Liberals and in particular the Prime Minister. Asquith was not in favour of any change in the status of women's voting rights, and hundreds of posters and postcards were printed showing 'Double faced Asquith'.

On one hand public opinion was outraged and sickened by suffragette militancy, but on the other it deplored the treatment of suffragette prisoners.

Perhaps there was a certain inevitability about the cause and eventually women had to be given the vote. Despite, however, a measure in 1918 whereby women over thirty could vote, it was not until 1928, the year that Mrs. Pankhurst died, when women over the age of twenty-one were included on the electoral role. Through a series of Parliamentary Acts the legal position of women had slowly altered.

I have been amazed at the sacrifice and lengths to which women, Christian or not, have been prepared to go in order to establish change. I can understand the anger of some women who feel that the Bible has been used to justify women's subjugation. Despite accusations from inside the Church that Christian feminists are simply following the world, I would suggest that the Church has mimicked society's attitudes towards women for almost 2000 years.

With God all things are possible

We have an enormous task if we want to see historical trends reversed. The odds appear overwhelming at times, as we battle against 2000 years of history. I believe, however, that with our God, this is truly possible.

We all suffer from feelings of inferiority, but perhaps women are more susceptible, hardly surprising in view of the oppression and subjugation they have experienced. A couple of years ago I was invited to speak at a Christian conference. I was the only woman speaker. As each of the speakers shared, not only did they talk of their successes, but none appeared to have doubts or difficulties in their ministry. Their lives seemed to be full of victory, confidence and unabated blessing. I didn't see a chink of weakness in their armour.

I returned to my room that night and thought for a long time about what I had heard. What more could I add to that show of strength? My ministry was certainly not like theirs. I sat up until 3am, wondering if my own message had any validity at all. Did I have anything worthwhile to say? Had I really heard God with respect to what I was hoping to say the next day? Eventually I knelt down and simply asked God to restore my confidence and belief in what He had given me. My prayer was answered. The following morning I woke with a new assurance in my heart that God had given me His word to share. After I had spoken, a number of people approached me and confirmed this. This experience, together with many others taught me that feelings of inferiority can be overcome by prayer and an act of the will. This choice is made easier when we become aware of the negative forces which are at work in us and, having recognised them, work at being liberated from them. Jesus has given us the power and authority to 'set the captives free' (Isaiah 61.1; Matthew 10.1).

Model from the past

I recently commented to a colleague that the history of women was a fascinating subject. He answered me by saying: 'Yes, they have been around a long time.' My response was, 'At first glance you would not think so!'

The history of women, especially those in the church has been poorly documented, and few studies are readily available. My research has been rewarding, however, and I am profoundly grateful to God for those women who have been willing to blaze a trail and shine as examples of 'what can be'.

In the fifteenth century the mother of Henry VII, Margaret Beaufont, received no formal education, but she could read and write English and understand French. Inspired by the new spirit of learning during the Renaissance, Margaret founded Jesus College, Cambridge in 1496 and Christ College, Cambridge in 1505. In the light of this it is ironic that women were only granted degrees there in 1948.

Mary Astor founded a school and seminary of her own in the mid 1700s. She was concerned that women should be educated and she made a stand against arranged marriages which were still found at almost every level of society. Miss Astor planned to provide a college of higher education for '. . . the most neglected part of the world – the ladies.'

Part of the spiritual awakening of the eighteenth and nineteenth centuries saw the formation of the Salvation Army. General William Booth said, 'My best men are women.' There are some other outstanding examples of women who strove to challenge the pervading trends of the Church in their day. Florence Nightingale, one of the best known examples, sensed the call of God on her life at the age of seventeen, but was unsure exactly to what. She said of the Church, 'I would have given the church my head, my heart, my hand. She would not have them. She told me to go back to crochet in my mother's drawing room or marry and look well at the head of my husband's table.' Internationally known as the founder of modern nursing, she went to the battle front of the Crimean War at the request of Sydney Herbert, the Minister of War, and became known as 'the angel of the Crimea'. She reduced the death rate from 42 per cent to 2.2 per cent in six months.

Returning to England she began to re-organise the army medical service, and with money given to her for her work in the Crimea, she founded the first training school for nurses at St. Thomas' Hospital in London. She devoted herself solely to her work and in 1907 became the first woman to be awarded the British Order of Merit.

Already mentioned in a previous chapter, Mary Slessor, a missionary of the United Presbyterian Church, served in West Africa for 39 years and was respected by the local people to the extent that she could bring to an end many tribal abuses including twin murder, human sacrifice, witchcraft and cruelty.

In more recent times, the late Kathryn Kuhlman exercised one of the most powerful public teaching and healing ministries ever seen in the United States of America. Other noteworthy examples include Dr. Henrietta Mears, a great American Bible teacher, Corrie Ten Boom, who survived internment in the Nazi concentration camps and Jackie Pullinger who has shown courage, faith and love in ministering to people in the 'Walled City' of Kowloon, Hong Kong, establishing a thriving church there.

There are countless others I could mention. I do not have time to tell about Deborah, Ruth, Esther, Huldah,

Anna and Priscilla, who through faith conquered kingdoms, administered justice, and gained what was promised. The world was not worthy of them. (Adapted from Hebrews 11).

I now have a profound sense of gratitude and admiration for these pioneers, women who have blazed a trail for others to follow. Their lives clearly demonstrate that if a woman desires to serve God, He will make a way for her to do so. Let us take courage from the examples of those who have persevered and endured against the odds, settling for nothing less than the full release of women into the roles for which they are intended.

7: . . . Our Destiny

What seems to be a contemporary issue is not only linked with our history, both personal and general, but also the destiny of all Christians and ultimately the world. Many people appreciate the enormous difficulties faced by women in the twentieth century church, but few have found credible answers or resolutions to these problems. The most secure foundation from which to start is a firm grasp of God's ultimate plan for men and women and an idea of how he will restore his ideal for the future.

If it is important for us to know our history, it is perhaps more so to know our destiny. Galatians chapter 3 verse 26 to chapter 4 verse 7 paints a picture of Christ's intentions for His Church: 'You are all sons of God through faith in Christ Jesus, for all of you who were baptised into Christ have clothed yourselves with Christ. There is neither Jew nor Greek, slave nor free, male nor female, for you are all one in Christ Jesus. If you belong to Christ, then you are Abraham's seed, and heirs according to the promise.

What I am saying is that as long as the heir is the child, he is no different from a slave, although he owns the whole estate. He is subject to guardians and trustees until the time set by his father. So also, when we were children, we were in slavery under the basic principles of the world. But when the time had fully come, God sent his Son, born of a woman, born under the law, to redeem those under law, that we might receive the full rights of sons. Because you are sons, God sent the Spirit of his Son into our hearts, the Spirit who calls out, "Abba, Father". So you are no longer a slave, but a son; and since you are a son, God has made you also an heir.'

Galatians has been called 'The Charter of Christian Liberty', because whilst describing the implications of grace on our behaviour, Paul strongly defends a Christian freedom which transcends Jewish law. He does this in response to Jewish legalists who had been insisting that non-Jewish converts to Christianity must be circumcised and observe Jewish law. In other words they were saying, 'Unless you are Jewish you cannot be truly saved.' This has an ominous ring to it.

In real terms this approach was a death blow to God's free gift of salvation and would have had far-reaching implications for other aspects of Christian life. Paul explains that Jesus fulfilled the promise given to Abraham (Genesis 12.7; 13.15; 24.7), but *all christians* become joint heirs in Christ.

Paul's statements were certainly controversial! He hammered home the basis of our acceptance to God by faith alone, not by works, religion or any other value system.

First he challenged racial attitudes. 'There is neither Jew nor Greek . . .' All racial barriers had been torn down by the work of Christ on the cross, and His resurrection. Jews and Gentiles, of course, still existed but the distinction was of little consequence in the Church of Jesus Christ. They were to live, eat and work together to demonstrate that Christ had redeemed them from the curse of the law (Galatians 3.13), and they were to show that fact to a watching world by their visible unity.

Paul then extends this freedom and unity to cover the many kinds of people in the Church. 'There is neither slave nor free . . .' he said, dispelling social, economic and inherited barriers in Christ. Slaves, considered to be one of the lower life forms of Paul's day, were given new value. Firstly, they were to be accepted into the Church as people for whom Christ had died, and, therefore, of inestimable value to God. Secondly, they were to be seen as equals to their brethren who were free citizens.

Paul supports this statement in practice when writing to Philemon about his runaway slave Onesimus. He entreats Philemon to welcome Onesimus home as a brother. He then concludes the triplet with: 'there is neither male nor female', literally 'male and female'. Sexual differences were to play no part in determining a person's status in the Church. Male dominance and superiority was at an end. Christ's life and death had once and for all dealt with the inequality that existed between the sexes. The standing of a woman was no longer to be linked with that of a man. Her identity and status sprung from her standing in Christ, an individual who had partaken of the life of Christ.

Paul's words did not eradicate the differences between the sexes, but changed the inter-relationship between them. The differences, in Christ, would be of little consequence, as they would no longer be differences of value.

Paul flings wide the door for women, as well as for Gentiles and slaves, to be accepted fully into the body of Christ as equal members, to find their role in the Church, use their gifts and abilities, and even exercise leadership where appropriate. Distinctions made at the time by the Jewish synagogue, Roman law, or society at large, were no longer relevant in the Church. Distinctions ceased to exist. Discrimination was over. Absolute equality was the order of the day.

Some have questioned Paul's emphasis on the first category – 'Jew nor Greek' – and his reason for mentioning the other two only in passing. Some scholars reply that there appears to have been no opposition in the early church to women or slaves having equal status, and it was therefore, an issue which Paul did not have to labour too much. Women were engaged in all types of ministry, including evangelism, teaching, leadership, diaconate and use of the spiritual gifts. There was no need for Paul to emphasise the point. Considerable evidence exists for the extent of male/female equality in New Testament times. A brief look at the list of co-workers whom Paul greeted in Romans chapter sixteen shows ten women who were aggressively engaged in the work of the ministry alongside Paul. They were not inferior to him, but were addressed as co-workers, people who worked with him, not for him.

There is little doubt that we have lost sight of the value of these verses. In the Church of Jesus Christ today, equality of status is largely still a dream. Sometimes I think, in my less hopeful moments, that women will only be fully released after Christ's return, but since Christians are people for whom the new age has already dawned, the powers of the new age in Christ are available to us now. We have the task of seeing Christ's kingdom established in our generation, and making real the age to come in the midst of this present one. Whether this will be fulfilled in our lifetime or not, is debatable, but there has to be a generation that will be bold and flexible enough to see it happen. I believe that Christ will not return for half a Bride, and women being released into their full potential is a necessary part of the preparation for his return.

I have already mentioned that a Jew would thank God that he had not been born a Gentile, a slave or a woman. Perhaps it is no accident that Paul reverses this prayer, and in fact takes this traditional saying and turns it upside down! The Jews would certainly have known precisely where Paul was aiming his arrows. It was no longer of any consequence whether a person was a Jew or barbarian, a slave or a free person, a man or a woman. What did matter was that all those who are in Christ become sons, and if sons, then heirs also.

Equality of status in Christ does not mean we have to become sexless, colourblind, or unaware of our differences. It means, however, that when we belong to Christ, distinctions do not disqualify us. We belong to Him and no-one can separate us from Him. Paul says that in the world of childhood, law holds sway. Before we become Christians, the law ruled us, but when Christ came, He released us from its tyranny. We are now no longer slaves of the law, but children who have already entered their inheritance. Freedom of manhood, as symbolised by the freedom enjoyed by Jewish boys on reaching their twelfth birthday, has come for all, both men and women. In that same sense we are all 'sons' and receive all the benefits accorded to 'sons'. It is a concept which heralds a new equality in status and function. Jesus has instituted a new value system in which religious, social and sexual differences play no part.

Our inheritance

If we are heirs, then what do we inherit? Our inheritance was encompassed in the land of Canaan, the land 'flowing with milk and honey': abundance, provision, rest for certain, but also much more besides.

In the New Testament there is greater revelation of the meaning of this inheritance. We are told that we will inherit the Kingdom of God (Matthew 5.3, 10); the earth (Matthew 5.5); salvation (Hebrews 1.14); a blessing (Peter 3.9); glory (Romans 8.17–18); and incorruption (1 Corinthians 15.50).

We also catch a glimpse of our future as heirs. There is a marvellous scene portrayed in the book of Revelation, where the elders and living creatures have prostrated themselves before the Lamb of God, and are singing a new song:

'. . . with your blood you purchased "men and women" for God from every tribe and language and people and nation. You have made them to be a kingdom and priests to serve our God, and they will reign on the earth' (Revelation 5.9–10).

Ultimately, of course, our inheritance will not be completed until the second coming of Christ. The book of Revelation tells us that the person who overcomes will enter the kingdom of God and become a son, but that does not mean that many of the blessings of our inheritance are not to be enjoyed now. If we are to be a reflection of this coming new age, and reign as brothers and sisters together, then at the very least we should be progressing towards that goal now.

There have been times when certain people have actively discouraged or tried to hinder me from ministering and fulfilling my role as a leader. On one occasion during a public meeting I felt constrained to pray for a member of the congregation, and moved towards them to do so. As I made my way, a gentleman swooped over to me from his side of the hall and, by blocking my path with his arm, prevented me from praying with the person. I tried again and the same thing happened. There was a gasp around the room, and I felt humiliated. Later I was able to take time to talk it through with the Lord and some friends, and the discomfort, embarrassment and humiliation I had felt was replaced once again by a sense of dignity and purpose. I was given fresh courage to continue by reminding myself of my inheritance.

We have a positive hope for the future because of events of nearly two thousand years ago. It is not only our hope of eternal salvation for the future but also our inheritance to be joint heirs with Christ, which begins now. Feelings of inferiority, inadequacy, rejection and pain cannot simply be overcome by 'just getting on with it'. We need new confidence that our inheritance is real, and belongs to every single one of us, male or female.

Our freedom

'Then you will know the truth, and the truth will set you free' (John 8.32). 'It is for freedom that Christ has set us free'. (Galatians 5.1). 'You, my brothers, were called to be free' (Galatians 5.13).

The cry from the heart of many women is 'let me be free!' But according to these verses of Scripture, a follower of Jesus already has freedom. So what kind of freedom did Jesus actually give to women?

I have already said that Jesus broke every cultural pattern that militated against women playing a full part in the kingdom of God. He set a precedent by his treatment of womankind and the value he ascribed to them. He also gave clear examples through his own ministry as to how they should be treated.

The story of the crippled woman in Luke chapter 13 is one of those instances. Jesus was prepared to heal a woman on the Sabbath day, and in so doing, to violate Jewish law. The synagogue leader rebuked the people for even contemplating their own healing on the Sabbath, but Jesus, referring to the woman he had healed called her 'a daughter of Abraham' (verse 16). This is significant because the phrase 'daughter of Abraham' is almost unknown in Jewish writings. 'Son of Abraham' was a common phrase, particularly when an individual's status in the community was being emphasised. Jesus sends a clarion call to men and women when he uses this title for a woman. In effect he was saying, 'Gentlemen, this woman is your equal'.

The account recorded in Matthew chapter 9 and Luke chapter 8 of the woman who had been bleeding for twelve years is also worthy of note. In Jewish society, a menstruating woman and those she touched were regarded as unclean (Leviticus 15.25–27). Imagine the isolation and loneliness this woman must have felt, having been regarded as unclean for the whole of that time. She should not have been in the crowd, and certainly not touching Jesus. When she did, however, far from rebuking her, He gave her His full attention, encouraged her and affirmed her faith. One can understand why, in view of society's attitudes towards her condition, it was with trembling that she told her story in public. Having commended her faith, and allowed an 'unclean' woman to touch Him, Jesus did not consider himself contaminated. He pointed the way to new attitudes and practices towards women.

Jesus' attitude towards the woman who had lived a sinful life, and who anointed Jesus at Bethany is retold in all four Gospels (Matthew 26; Mark 14; Luke 7 and John 12): 'When a woman who had lived a sinful life in that town learnt that Jesus was eating at the Pharisee's house, she brought an alabaster jar of perfume, and as she stood behind him at his feet weeping, she began to wet his feet with her tears. Then she wiped them with her hair, kissed them and put perfume on them.'

Despite the incredulity of some of the other guests, Jesus does nothing to stop the woman. In front of everyone He confirms His forgiveness of her, comments on her deep love and commends her faith. His response is one of gentleness and compassion towards her. He upholds the dignity and respect of a woman from whom most 'respectable' people in the town would have shied away. In one fell swoop he destroys every preconceived notion amongst people who were assembled for the meal.

In these last two instances, and there are many others, Jesus not only allowed women to touch him, but made a point of never excluding those of dubious repute. The woman at the well of Sychar and Mary Magdalene are but two examples. Jesus demonstrated His fulfillment of the Law and made the old purification rights for men and women unnecessary. Gender was no longer important. Faith in the Messiah was the overriding factor. Women were in no way to be restricted, isolated or excluded simply because they were female.

Our responsibility

On one occasion Jesus had been teaching on demonology and a woman cried out, '. . . Blessed is the mother who gave birth and nursed you!' He replied, 'Blessed rather are those who hear the word of God and obey it' (Luke 11.27–28).

This was no harsh rebuke from Jesus. The woman was simply reflecting an attitude held by women of her day. There was cause to be proud of having borne such a man. Perhaps if we were to put her words in twentieth century idiom, she would have said, 'I wish I could have been the one to give birth to You and raise You.' Jesus, however, showed her that there was a blessing which surpassed even that.

The significance of His response would have been understood then, but we may easily miss it. The fact that He responded to the woman at all would have been regarded as unique. Rabbis did not teach women, as we have already seen. But Jesus does more than simply acknowledge her. In effect He says that an even greater blessing is to be given to all women who are obedient to God, whatever that might entail. The very fact that women travelled with Jesus at all was unusual, since as far as teaching was concerned, women were *persona non grata*. Luke records the names of Mary, Joanna and Suzanna with those of the disciples. It would seem that Luke regarded them equal with the men, a marked departure from the traditional Jewish view of women as too insignificant to mention.

Jesus accepted financial provision from the women, and even more unusual for a rabbi, He allowed them to serve Him at table. He considered women to be among his closest friends, often visiting the house of Mary, Martha and Lazarus. He commended the service and ministry of women. In the gospel of Mark, we find him citing a widow as an example to His disciples. She had given to the temple treasury out of her poverty, and Jesus praised her sacrificial act, His response to the disciples being: 'This is how to do it' (Mark 12.41 ff). Jesus also uses a woman to illustrate persistence in the parable concerning the justice of God (Luke 18.1–8), and commends the faith of a Syro-Phoenician woman (Mark 7.28–30).

The significance of Jesus' response and actions towards women cannot be underestimated and although it would have been understood in the culture of His own time, we are in danger of underestimating or even overlooking it. Jesus broke every negative pattern of behaviour towards the down-trodden, including women. He not only replaced them with a new set of standards but provided an alternative basis from which all men and women can operate, that of equality with one another, in principle and in practice.

Jesus is said to have 'set His face like flint' towards Jerusalem. He knew the suffering that lay before Him, but He was determined to carry out the commission given to Him by His Father. A flower strewn pathway was never promised to His followers, but His example and that of so many men and women since has shown us that our suffering has a purpose. In the light of this the difficulties are bearable, for we have a hope denied to those outside Christ. We have a guaranteed inheritance which will not fade.

Christ laid the foundation upon which everyone may become mature and fulfil their potential. He left others to set the pace, and pursue his revolutionary departure from the patriarchal system that had been established through Judaism by the time that he was born.

Our responsibility is to call men and women to return to the principles established by Jesus. 'Suffering' may ensue in the sense of misunderstanding, opposition or rejection, but we have the example of Jesus to follow. I want to encourage all women and men to persevere with the work God has given them to do. Nothing else will fulfil in quite the same way. As the psalmist says:

'Lord, you have assigned me my portion and my cup; you have made my lot secure. The boundary lines have fallen for me in pleasant places; surely I have a delightful inheritance' (Psalm 16.5–6).

8: Every Man, Every Woman

We are currently enjoying a restoration of the plurality of leadership in many of the new churches. This is a refreshing change from the days when leaders did everything themselves. From the beginning, partnership was God's ideal, not exclusively the co-operation of women, but a complementary partnership of men and women working together, 'Then God said, "Let us make man in our image, in our likeness, and let them rule over the fish of the sea and the birds of the air, over the livestock over all the earth, and over all the creatures that move along the ground." (Genesis 1.26) In our local church we have discovered some key principles in male/female partnership, and continue to explore the differences women can bring to leadership.

I am convinced that men and women work best in partnership with each other and this includes their involvement in the Church. This was very clearly God's intention at the beginning of man's existence, and will be so in the new era to come at Christ's return.

In the Garden of Eden, man and woman were given joint responsibility to rule. Despite different functions, they were both given tasks. It is therefore quite reasonable to assume that God endowed both of them with the qualities necessary to fulfil that task. Woman was not subordinate or inferior to man in the beginning and neither will she be when Jesus comes again.

God's original intention was for men and women to form a fulfilling partnership to accomplish their work together. This is not restricted to the marriage relationship, but is open to all brothers and sisters in Christ. A special bonding of love and deep respect mentioned many times in the New Testament exists between those who know the Lord. In many of his letters Paul encourages believers to care for one another, honour one another, be devoted to one another, prefer one another, love one another, share with one another and pray for one another. How, then should this be worked out in practice?

We obviously need to be aware of the potential psychological and emotional risks when men and women work together. Some men feel inferior if asked to work with women – perhaps it threatens their manhood? Some women feel inferior without cause.

No matter how mature we imagine we are, and how strong we may feel, sexual temptation is always a danger. When two people work together towards a common goal, face struggles achieving it, and overcome difficulties, an emotional bonding is bound to occur. If one of the team feels low or vulnerable and receives emotional support lacking perhaps at home, over-involvement is always a possibility. The step from genuinely caring to sexual involvement is an easy step and sadly there are more ministers and leaders than we would like to admit who can testify to that fact.

No legislation can protect us from venturing over boundaries we must not cross, for everyone is tempted, and temptation is no respecter of rules. Our protection and safety must be in forming deep relationships, some of which need to be outside the working relationship where we can share openly and honestly about our struggles in this area. We must have this kind of forum, so that we have people we are able to go to when we are tempted. Clearly it would be unhelpful to go to the person with whom we have the problem because we could easily create an even bigger one. Many have discovered that once a temptation is aired openly the threat of immorality is largely dealt with before the temptation has had time to take root. It has to be said, nevertheless, that only by God's grace can any us avoid these pitfalls.

Men and women often over-react towards each other with feelings of hostility, fear and anger, for no apparent reason. I believe that this is often because the forces of darkness have a vested interest in maintaining division and enmity between the sexes, in order to pervert the will of God for unity and equality. The New Testament clearly states that Jesus paid the necessary price to redeem us from the dichotomy of the dominant and submissive sexes.

We see in Scripture that God wants us all to live and work together in harmony. We are told to: 'submit to one another' (Ephesians 5.21), words spoken in the general context of Christian living. We are commanded to: 'consider others better than yourselves' (Philippians 2.3). Looking at the general tenor of the New Testament, these and other comments make it clear that men should not think of themselves as better or superior to women, nor are they more fitted for ministry or leadership.

Since I began to lead a church, I have had the opportunity to develop my own style, innovate, initiate, and explore different ways of leading. In the past the newer churches have reacted against an entirely democratic way of government, feeling that plans and ideas were never able to be implemented at a reasonable pace, and also that it did not truly reflect the biblical style of leadership. Unfortunately, in some cases, having rejected the democratic way, what seemed to happen was that this was replaced with an autocratic form of government, which was no more Scriptural.

I attended a leadership conference where delegates were asked to fill out a questionnaire to help determine their style of leadership. My dominant leadership style was assessed as being equally 'directive' and 'democratic'. The comment I received was, 'A very unusual mix, and one that would be interesting to observe in practice!'

The style I am finding myself increasingly comfortable with is that of consensus. This can make people feel insecure on the one hand because some want strong leadership to make all the decisions for them, but on the other, people can be included in the decision making process, which makes them feel their opinions count and that they are able to contribute constructively. I believe in leadership through relationship, endeavouring to gain the confidence of people, and behaving with integrity towards them.

Encouragement from others has helped me to bring my own style to leadership. One man came to me and said, 'I still have a problem with the idea of women in church leadership, but I can see the positive results of your ministry.' Such comments have helped my confidence. There has been no substitute, however, for believing that my own personality, talents and abilities are not only important to God, but also to his Church.

I can only lead by trusting that God has given me something to share with others. If the need to be convinced of our own value, and our opinions is a universal phenomenon, it is certainly more acute for women. Fortunately God is not limited by our own estimation of ourselves, and does not wait for all our problems to be sorted out before he uses us. The processes of healing and serving run side by side.

There are probably as many different styles of leadership as there are leaders. We are all unique and I could not begin to describe the 'typical' male leader. Generalising a little here, I would say that their positive characteristics include: clarity in pointing the way forward; the ability to stand firm during times of uncertainty; inspiring confidence in others and a willingness to be direct when necessary. On the other hand there tends to be a tendency towards task-centredness, inflexibility, over lengthy deliberation on issues and the desire to dominate.

As far as the typical leading woman is concerned, there are still very few female leaders from whom to gain a picture. From those that I know, positive attributes include a clear desire for servanthood; perception that sees behind the issues; and a sensitivity in dealing with people. On the negative side, however, they sometimes feel insecure, inferior, lack confidence and have a tendency to retaliate if cornered. Perhaps sisterhood will be more difficult to achieve than brotherhood.

I agree with Dave Tomlinson leader of Teamwork, a group of men and women based in the Brixton area of London who care for a number of New Churches, when he says, 'We want partnership, not an exchange of power.' Jesus restored this fundamental principle between men and women in the kingdom of God when He was alive on Earth, but it was soon lost again after He ascended to heaven. His radical nature seems to manifest itself during revivals, when there is renewed concern for the poor and oppressed in the community, a loss of religiosity, and new life restored to God's people. This often includes the release of resources that have been lying dormant for a long time, one of which is women.

Revivals come and go, but the new kingdom of the Lord Jesus will last forever. I believe He will return to the generation of His Bride, where His children have learnt to work together in harmony; where social, racial and sexual divides will have been dismantled; where there will still be differences but no division. Unity of this kind is of the utmost importance, and must be high on our agenda. If we do not work for this kind of oneness and harmony we will not fulfil the heartcry of God's Son for unity amongst his followers.

There is no doubt that in order to establish women in joint leadership with men a number of issues will have to be confronted. The area of brother/sister relationships will require some attention, so that wives do not become nervous when their husbands are with a female leader. There will need to be a heightened awareness of the way men treat women, albeit subconsciously, and the reasons for this. A greater willingness to confess weaknesses and strengths to each other will also be necessary and we will all need our eyes opened to subconscious prejudices.

These are not easy issues to look at, and will certainly require much time, effort and patience to work through. If that is what is required, let us endeavour not to shrink from the task, so that in the future all women will be free to realise their potential.

The Lord wants us to be partners together and to have committed relationships. In our society there is a tendency for men and women to over-react to one another. At one extreme we have the male chauvinist, and at the other the radical feminist. I believe there could be no more powerful an example of what is possible between the sexes for our own society, than that it sees men and women working together in harmony in all areas of church life, each fulfilling their potential to the full, and working in a harmonious atmosphere of interdependence.

I have already mentioned that as Christians we are inextricably linked with a special type of bond, a unique love between brothers and sisters, which our enemies are dedicated to divide. In the same way that it is true that enmity was placed between Satan and woman because from her would come the Saviour of the world, it is also true that Jesus triumphed over these enemies and that they are aware that all other children born of women may be potential victims over Satan's power. One of Satan's strategies is to keep the people of the earth from a relationship with God. If he cannot do that, he will prevent Christians from being effective by any means possible. Our spiritual enemies have a vested interest in keeping women subservient, inferior, rejected and therefore unused assets of the Church.

The victory at the cross was so remarkable that it would take many lifetimes to comprehend. In His new kingdom, Jesus will make us stand complete in Him. Then we shall be like Him, for we shall see Him as He really is. For the time being we see but a poor reflection. We need each other to complement each other, and until we truly grasp that fact, I believe the church will only function on half its power, and will never make the impact in society that God longs for.

The devil wants to maintain the division between the sexes. Jesus, however, has given us the ministry of reconciliation, and wherever there is division between people, whether rich and poor, black and white, male and female, we are charged to transform the enmity into friendship. It is vital that we do not provoke and antagonise one another, which could so often lead to misunderstanding and separation, but rather we should seek to understand one another's perspectives, with open minds and hearts towards each other, knowing that the perspectives of the other person may be just as valid as our own.

Men and women who dare to work together in leadership by submitting to each other are still in a minority and it is a struggle, of that there is little doubt. But the struggle exists not because it is wrong but because it is giving birth to something new; the intense desire to bring about truth, reality, reconciliation and life.

Amongst the New Churches ten years ago, there were no women in key positions of leadership. Today the tide is beginning to turn, even if the process is painfully slow. Some women have been accepted into areas of leadership; others have been invited to serve on leadership teams, and a handful are actually leading churches. By God's grace I am one of those few. I have arrived at that position without the help and support of a husband, although I must stress that I have not made it on my own. If I can do it, I know beyond a shadow of a doubt that others can, if they are only given a chance.

People often say to me, 'I felt alright until I became a Christian.' Perhaps they mean that once they submitted to the Lordship of Jesus, things began to change as the very core of their being was shaken. As the Spirit of God points out areas in our lives that He wants to change, this can be uncomfortable. Where women begin to pioneer and cut across the grain of our society, our culture, two thousand years of Christian teaching, and a history of oppression, they too will find breaking free an uncomfortable experience. Only through the grace of Christ at work within us will this be accomplished. May God grant us all the ability to receive His grace in order to find the freedom that Jesus has bought for us and see it established in this generation.

Postscript: By Peter Brayne

I want to describe my experience of working with women in ministry and more particularly being apprenticed into my leadership role by Brenda Robson. There are many influences in life which cause us to change and may help us to mature, but there is no doubt that for the last two years, the person who has most influenced my development is Brenda. Although these experiences are personal, I trust they have a more general application.

Brenda and my family had been friends for several years but I first saw her leadership qualities in action when she led a counselling course. I was struck not only by her insight and understanding, but also by her single-minded determination to grow in God. Soon after this Brenda started to meet with a small group of women. This was not only a 'prayer and share' group, but an opportunity for women to express some of their deepest difficulties. They encouraged each other and miracles of healing took place. It was not long before the positive results in their lives became obvious.

Soon there were three of these groups. Although I do not think that I ever heard it actually said by the men, there was a feeling that 'It was good that our women were getting themselves sorted out!' The crunch came when Brenda suggested that perhaps the men needed to 'get themselves sorted out too!'

Eventually ten men, including myself, were invited to take part in a similar group; but who was to lead us in this new field? We all recognised there was only one person who could and that was Brenda – 'But she was a woman!'. I have to admit the big question in most of our minds at that time was not so much a theological one, but, 'What happens if the problem I want to share is a sexual one?' The implication was that women cannot possibly understand these areas and confiding in them might cause even more difficulties.

At our first meeting, we really did not know how the group was going to work, but we believed that the best person to lead us was Brenda. Despite the fact that she was a woman, we would give it a go. Brenda was prepared to risk a great deal in order that God could use her where He wanted to. She brought to us an understanding of feelings and enabled us to be set free from many long standing difficulties. We became aware of parts of our lives which needed release and healing. We experienced major changes in our lives, made possible through the perceptions given to a woman.

Through this group I discovered a principle which has been continually reinforced through the years and that is:

> A woman's perspective and perceptions are necessary to bring men into maturity.

The reverse obviously is true too. The truth is we need each other in order to be released. A fixation with single sex groups can polarise attitudes and feelings into 'gender corners', flexing their muscles and so fuelling the fight between the sexes.

Brenda began to apprentice me to lead the group. I was willing to be apprenticed (trained in action), but at the same time lacked confidence and was aware of the tough act I had to follow! Brenda never forced me to lead if I did not feel able, but was a great encourager.

Brenda led by example. One of the principles to which she had stuck doggedly over the years is, 'in order to help others, you must first be helped yourself'. And so it was that she would submit to the group and share her weaknesses in order to receive God's strength through us. This brings me to another general principle which I have found to be true:

'Women often lead in the area of submission.'

In some ways this may seem a contradiction in terms, but in the light of the way Jesus led, I feel it fully accords with Scripture.

In 1983 Terry Brewer, who had been in full time Christian leadership for several years, began to lead Guildford Community Church and needed to build his own team. Brenda naturally became Terry's senior partner among us. As in the life of any church, we have faced our fair share of opposition. One of these attacks was directed against Brenda and was designed to undermine her ministry. The nature of the difficulty, however, meant that she was the best qualified to confront the people concerned. She handled the situation superbly, and despite the considerable emotional pain, was able to be objective and see the matter through to a conclusion.

I saw then that women can be strong. If there is any truth in a woman's emotional vulnerability, it is not an inherent, irreversible female weakness, but rather produced by forces at work within our male dominated society. Although this domination often inflicts wounds upon women, when God heals, these very same areas can become those of great strength. My principle is

'The hardship and struggle women endure often produces great strength of character.'

Towards the beginning of 1988, Brenda assumed the leadership of our church. I became the second most experienced person in leadership. The responsibility for my apprenticeship became unreservedly Brenda's because she was my Team Leader and ultimately responsible for the whole church. We are colleagues and therefore spend much time working together on diverse areas of church life.

'What's it been like?', you might ask. It is unlikely that I would criticise her apprenticeship of me – after all it is her book! The truth however, is that I would not be writing this chapter if I did not passionately believe that Brenda has something important to share and this has been tested and proven through many years.

As I have already mentioned it is difficult to formulate general principles concerning women in leadership from the way that Brenda has tackled the job. What I have done is to list a number of important features describing the way Brenda has apprenticed me. I will leave it for you to decide whether they find an agreement in your heart concerning women in general.

First, Brenda has always shown that she is concerned for me as a person and for my family above what I do. She wants to know how we all are, my wife Val and two sons, Jonathan and Tim. She will even on occasion, invite herself around for supper to ensure that her relationship with the rest of the family is maintained.

Second, she cares enough to confront. No doubt one of the most difficult tasks of a leader. She does not easily let me ignore aspects of my character which need to be changed (i.e. those areas which have a detrimental influence on my effectiveness for God and personal well-being).

Third, she has great tenacity and an eye for detail. When I am ready to quit and would rather ignore specific situations, she will press on. Instead of giving up, she will enable us to find a way through the situation together. By direction and encouragement she ensures that God's purpose is achieved.

Fourth, she is a woman of integrity. By this I do not mean that she adheres legalistically to truth, but that she possesses the quality of 'being true'. She has a strong desire to be honest in every respect, in word, deed and feelings. I have never heard Brenda gossip.

This may sound as though I am the chairman of the Brenda Robson Fan Club'. In a way I am, but equally I am not oblivious to her weaknesses and failings. Like all of us, she needs others with their different gifts and perspectives to help and support her.

Brenda has included in her team both men and women. I am privileged to be one of the men in her team. I sometimes ask myself, 'What would it be like if I were excluded from such a team because I am a man?!'

Bibliography

Atkins, Anne *Split Image* (Hodder and Stoughton)
Attalah, Naim *Woman* (Quartet Books)
Beard, Helen *Women in Ministry Today* (Logos International)
Black, Hugh B. *A Trumpet Call to Women* (New Dawn Books)
Brand, Jean *A Woman's Privilege*, (SPCK/Triangle)
Briscoe, Jill *Queen of Hearts* (Kingsway Publications)
Evans, Eifion *Revivals: Their Rise, Progress and Achievements* (Evangelical Press of Wales)
Evans, Mary J. *Women in the Bible* (The Paternoster Press)
Forster, Roger *The New Humanity* (Icthus Fellowship Pamphlet)
Finney, Charles Grandison *Finney on Revival* (Bethany House Publications)
Gray, Herbert *Men, Women and God* (Churchman Publishing)
General Synod of the Church of England *The Ordination of Women to the Priesthood. A second Report by the House of Bishops* (Church House)
Hagin, Kenneth *The Woman Question* (Faith Library Publications)
Hayter, Mary *The New Eve in Christ* (SPCK)
Houghton, S.M. *Sketches from Church History* (Banner of Truth)
Hurley, James B. *Man and Woman in Biblical Perspective* (Inter-Varsity Press)

Jewett, Paul K. *Man as Male and Female*
(Eerdmans Publishing)

Karssen, Glen *Her Name Is Woman* Books 1 and 2
(Navpress)

Keays, Kathy (ed.) *Men, Women and God*
(Marshall Pickering)

Lees, Shirley (ed.) *The Role of Women*
(Inter-Varsity Press)

Lloyd-Jones, D. Martin *Revival, can we make it happen?*
(Marshall Pickering)

Loades, Ann *Searching for Lost Coins* (SPCK)

Muler, Jean Baker *Towards a New Psychology of Women*
(Beacon Press)

Murrey, Ian H. (ed.) *The Reformation of the Church* – A collection of Reformed and Puritan documents on Church Issues. (Banner of Truth)

Penn-Lewis, Jessie *The Awakening in Wales*
(Overcomer Publications)

Pollock, John *George Whitefield and the Great Awakening*
(Lion Publishing)

Storkey, Elaine *What's right with Feminism* (SPCK)

Swindler, Leonard *Biblical Affirmations of Women*
(Westminster Press)

Tournier, Paul *The Gift of Feeling* (SCM Press)

Virgo, Wendy *Leading ladies* (Kingsway Publications)

Wallis, Eileen *Queen take your throne*
(Kingsway Publications)

Wesley, John *The nature of Revival*
(Bethany House Publications)

Whittaker, Colin *Great Revivals* (Marshall Pickering)

Williams, Don *The Apostle Paul and Women in the Church*
(Regal Books)

Wirt, Sherwood Eliot (ed.) *Spiritual Awakening,*
(Lion Publishing)